Landscape Poets

ROBERT BURNS

Landscape Poets

ROBERT BURNS

Selected and introduced by Karl Miller
Photographs by John Hedgecoe

Weidenfeld and Nicolson   London

First published in Great Britain by
George Weidenfeld and Nicolson Limited
91 Clapham High Street, London SW4 7TA

Designed by Allison Waterhouse

ISBN 0 297 77991 5

Printed in Great Britain by Butler & Tanner Ltd,
Frome and London

Contents

Introduction

This selection of poems by Burns is arranged according to theme, and the themes, in the order of their appearance, are these: art, friendship, religion, animals, drink, marriage, love. The first two and the last of all – poetry, sociability and sexual adventure, to call them by other names – commemorate activities which enabled him in youth, as did his drinking, to face the prospect of a lifetime's hard labour on the land. After just such a life, his own auld farmer addressed his auld mare in these words:

> Mony a sair darg we twa hae wrought,
> An' wi' the weary warl' fought!
> An' mony an anxious day I thought
> We wad be beat!
> Yet here to crazy age we're brought,
> Wi' something yet.

Burns himself was never to win through to crazy age, with its 'something yet': he died young, at the age of thirty-seven – *en pòete*, as he put it – of a rheumatic affliction of the heart caused or assisted, it would seem, both by work and by drink. So you could say that he was never anything but young, and that his youth was sustained by his art, his friends and his lovers.

His good poems are often about the experience of writing poetry, and of doing so with the wolf, and the factor, at the door. Poetry and poverty – his epistles are charged with that conjunction, and with the pleasures of male friendship. Male friendship, with its deep potations, divided him from women, and provided a setting in which women could be worshipped and insulted, and which sorted his poems of love and sexual adventure into two categories: some were seen to invite the lyre, the stance of nature's gentleman, the man of feeling, poor but honest and passionately sincere, while others are sincerely aggressive and derisive. Both kinds are segregational, so to speak, in that they seem to be assignable to a separate sex of convivial males, and to share in the consensus which is celebrated in the second of these seven themes.

This selection adores the epistolary Burns, and is more interested in the byre than the lyre. It is more interested in the poems he made up for himself and for his first friends about the tasks and pleasures they pursued together, and in the poems he wrote about his art and about its origins and occasions, than it is in those that came of his need to be a man of standing, and of feeling, in the metropolis of Edinburgh, by whose upper ranks this stranger from the wilds of the West could be worshipped and insulted – for bringing news of 'nature', and for bringing them a message from the poor, and, obliquely, from Paris, where the poor were starting a revolution. The selection has many of the pieces which are still known by heart to Scots people, and many of these are lyrical in character; it does not overlook his valuable activities as a defender of the oral and literate popular tradition in verse; there are poems here, such as 'The Lass of Ecclefechan', of which he is the collector as well as, or rather than, the author. Nevertheless, the emphasis is firmly epistolary. In the epistles, the life of the labouring poor, and of the men of parts numbered among their immediate superiors, in a corner of the country whose metropolis was Ayr, 'wham ne'er a town surpasses', is authentically and variously present. His powers of expression are at a high point of development, and are used in a wider variety of ways than they are elsewhere. Yet the epistles have usually been neglected in favour of other aspects of his work, and of conceptions of it which are more or less intolerant of the conversational mode.

I doubt myself, for example, whether 'The Jolly Beggars' deserves the central place which modern conceptions of the dramatic, and the impersonal, in art, and of a Brechtian Burns, have assigned to it. This 'cantata', in praise of 'Love and Liberty', is a version of pastoral which resembles other versions, which resembles Ramsay's *Gentle Shepherd*, in appearing to embody an urban view of country life. The rural Burns does much to authenticate the view with a bitterness and candour from which his beggars are not exempt, and to persuade the reader that the poem is valid, and was valid for Burns, as an attack on an oppressive and deceitful social system. But there is also the sense that the poem allows healthy and wealthy readers to play at outlaws, while consoling them with the thought that love and liberty must be paid for in rags and sores and stumps.[1]

Burns burns brightest when he treats the life of his first localities, the native ground to which he chose to return after his lionising in Edinburgh: many readers would agree with that. But what should any argument about Burns proceed to say next? Sooner or later it has to engage with certain divisions and distinctions which are evident in his poetry. A segregation of men and women has already been mentioned. Another division has to do with the difference between Scotland and England, and with the rivalry in his work between the languages, or dialects, of Scots and English: between the speech which he learnt in childhood and the speech which was heard in the south of the island, and which had come to be increasingly cultivated among eminent and ambitious Northerners. His attitude to the language question has been seen by compatriots as a measure of his Scottish patriotism: but it may well be more significant of his attitude to class. Not only nationality but also, and perhaps more especially, class were at issue in the choice he faced between Scots and English, and were expressed in the accommodations he reached between the two in forming a diction for his verse, in the shifts made, as he drove, between the one and the other. That he was a keen Scots patriot can't be denied, but the patriotism which we meet with on the page is as often as not regional in character, and at its most animated and expansive in dealing with members of his own class, who are apt to look like his true compatriots. While resenting its cruelties and injustice, moreover, he accepted the accomplished fact of a Hanoverian Britain – Jacobite and Jacobinical as he can sometimes by turns appear.

A traditional appreciation of his work has insisted that he was sound when he wrote in Scots on Scots subjects, unsound when he wrote with an eye on the Augustan inheritance, in which the ways of the Southern metropolis were preserved as an example to the world and an epitome of pre-romantic human nature; and that he was all for Scotland as opposed to England. But it is no less true that he felt himself to belong to a British literature, and that many of his favourite poets wrote in English. And, as Thomas Crawford has shown, much of the folk repertoire he studied was common to both the northern and southern halves of the island. It is also true that Scots and English are branches of the same language, and that Burns was not, in the customary meaning of the word, bilingual.[2]

A way into Burns's verse is opened up by 'The Vision', which is both a landscape poem and an account of his poetic vocation. Having returned one winter's day in depression and fatigue to his cottage or bigging, he is visited by Coila, the muse of an Ayrshire vicinity, the *genius loci* of the district of Kyle. A shortened text of the poem was included in the Kilmarnock edition of 1786, which made his name, though not his fortune, and sent him to Edinburgh. The poem is thought to have been composed at an earlier time or times – possibly as early as the hard time represented by the Burns family's tenancy of the farm at Lochlie, which came to an end, with his father's death, in 1784. W. P. Ker once said of it that it reverts to 'the old allegorical, didactic form', that 'there is some connection between Burns's "Vision" and the vision of Boethius.' James Kinsley's encyclopedic Oxford edition of the poems and songs has traced this connection, among others. The supernatural devices of Pope's *Rape of the Lock* are employed; the division of the poem into sections called Duans is drawn from Macpherson's *Ossian*. And the connection Ker looked for between Burns's 'Vision' and ancient literature is stated to be 'the frequent discussion of the Platonic *genius loci* and "intermediary spirits" in 17th-century letters', to which Pope, in particular, was later to be drawn.[3]

If this is a learned or literary poem, it wears its learning lightly. As such, nevertheless, it is very informative. In the midst of the soldiers and scholars who made up the local patriciate, it identifies the poets from the British beyond in whom Burns has been interested. Beattie, Thomson, Shenstone, Gray – the first two are Scottish poets who wrote wholly or mainly in English, and the others are English. The Scotsman Robert Fergusson, who meant far more to him than any of these and whom he discovered around 1784, is conspicuously omitted, though Kinsley detects the example of Fergusson in the scene-setting stanzas.

The author of the poem is in his mid-twenties, and has lang syne been in the habit of rhyming. His 'prime' has been passed in this way, and it all began at the age of fifteen, when love induced him to commit the 'sin', as he once put it, of writing verse.

> All in this mottie misty clime,
> I backward mused on wasted time,
> How I had spent my youthfu' prime,
>   An' done nae-thing,
> But stringin' blethers up in rhyme
>   For fools to sing.

> Had I to guid advice but harkit,
> I might, by this, hae led a market,
> Or strutted in a bank, and clarkit
>   My cash-account:
> While here, half-mad, half-fed, half-sarkit,
>   Is a' th'amount.

Burns excelled at a poetry of wit which is copious and brilliant in the epistles and which can sometimes be seen to follow the example of Pope: perhaps, in the second of these stanzas, there is a hint of the 'Epistle to Arbuthnot', in which a poet who had blethered in verse as a child, 'lisp'd in numbers', is bothered by poets who are poor, miserable and mad, who amount to nothing. For the purposes of wit, the Habbie Simpson stanza form, used in 'The Vision', is a vehicle which can on occasion serve almost as well as the heroic couplet.

Burns says here that so far in his life he has 'done nae-thing' except write poems, while the Lass of Ecclefechan complains elsewhere to her husband:

> Gat ye me, O gat ye me,
> O gat ye me wi' naething ...

Naething, or nothing, is a dimension (one among others which can often appear to contradict it) of the world Burns inhabited – a world of hard work, small leisure, subsistence living, rats in the roof, wolf at the door, girls in the gloaming or corn. In that world, as in his satire on Dr Hornbook, death was a sinister 'Something', which might be personified, and mitigated, in a poem. And poetry itself was a further something, a something out of nothing, comparable to the 'something yet' which had survived for his farmer in old age. It is no wonder that the creation of literature should have furnished him with a major theme. *Ex nihilo*, the poems and song of Burns.

In this respect and others, Burns is like a peasant poet of modern times, the Irishman Patrick Kavanagh, who spent many hard and lonely years as a farmer, and of whom Seamus Heaney, another Irish poet with close ties to the world of the countryside, has written: 'he wrested his idiom bare-handed out of a literary nowhere.' 'I am king,' wrote Kavanagh of himself in a beautiful poem, 'Of banks and stones and every blooming thing.'[4] 'Peasant poet' will look derogatory to some, and it is as well to add that the peasant's nowhere and nothing hardly characterise the work of Heaney, and are no more than an aspect of Kavanagh's work – or of that of Burns. Burns was, as Kinsley's edition demonstrates, a cultivated man, and no stranger to the Scottish Enlightenment.

The nothingness experienced by Burns is disclosed, in 'The Vision', by his 'half-sarkit' state. A 'sark' is a shirt. A 'cutty sark' is a short shirt, with mini-skirt features, and is worn by the witch Nannie in 'Tam o' Shanter'. Nannie's garment is therefore not all that different from the one worn by the poet in this poem. Playing with the word as he does, Burns manages to make poverty erotic while evoking the nothingness and naked-ness which turned him to love and lyre, and to a poetry of wit.

When Coila draws the string attached to the 'snick', lifts the latch, as it were, and enters his despondent cottage, she is clad in a televisual plaid on which moving pictures of the local landscape are registered. The garment suits her aerial status, but the robe beneath it shows a real leg. If Coila is a muse and a television screen, she is also an attractive girl, not unlike Nannie the witch: since love and poetry go together in Burns, and got started together, it may be that the witch and the muse have a sinful something in common.

> When click! the string the snick did draw;
> An' jee! the door gaed to the wa';
> And by my ingle-lowe I saw,
>> Now bleezin' bright,
> A tight outlandish hizzie, braw,
>> Come full in sight.

The drawing of the snick is a fateful action in Burns's poetry, and it may bear, as here, an erotic meaning. Satan performs the act in the 'Address to the Deil':

> Lang syne, in Eden's bonnie yard,
> When youthfu' lovers first were pair'd,
> And all the soul of love they shar'd,
>> The raptur'd hour,
> Sweet on the fragrant flow'ry swaird,
>> In shady bow'r;
>
> Then you, ye auld snick-drawing dog!
> Ye cam to Paradise incog.
> An' play'd on man a cursed brogue,
>> (Black be your fa!)
> An' gied the infant warld a shog,
>> 'Maist ruin'd a'.

It is a mark of Burns's genius that he makes what he does of the expression 'lang syne' – past times, long ago. He has the ability to make poverty erotic and to make the Fall of Man seem like something recollected at a silver wedding. The poem 'Auld Lang Syne' is one of his, or the folk tradition's, best:

> We twa hae paidled i' the burn,
>> From morning sun till dine;
> But seas between us braid hae roar'd
>> Sin' auld lang syne.

These lines belong with the auld farmer's words to his mare: here is a poetry of endurance, achieved by a master of the ephemeral.

To return to the hunting of sarks and snicks, Satan, the lifter of latches, is also glimpsed, in Burns, as a lifter of sarks. 'To a Mountain Daisy' has this, in Southern English, about the ploughing of the flower in its 'scanty mantle':

> Such is the fate of artless maid,
> Sweet flow'ret of the rural shade,
> By love's simplicity betray'd,
>   And guileless trust,
> Till she like thee, all soil'd, is laid
>   Low i' the dust.

Such, too, is the fate, says the next verse, of the luckless bard, of the author of the poem. Elsewhere in Burns's life and work, however, the devil who lays low trusting country girls is none other than Rab the Ranter himself. The story has been told (and may have been invented) in modern times of how Rab met a rural maid as they came through the rye. The rural maid spiered – inquired – his name, and having carefully established who he was, said with a sigh: 'I micht as weel lay doon ma basket.' The imagined scene may be effortlessly attached to the biographical record, to several items on one side of that ledger, and this accountancy confronts us with the difference between the commender of nymphs, the gifted and respectable unfortunate with his endowment of strong and fine feelings, and the by no means apocryphal coiner, connoisseur and actor-out of lines like 'Syne coup her o'er amang the creels.' There are poems in which the opposing conducts are in some sense reconciled, and the epistolary mode may be thought to have encouraged a convergence: but it is mostly a matter of one or the other, as indeed it had to be. It would be facile to claim that his scatology is sincere and his sensibility affected, and wrong to claim that his best poetry includes his contributions to *The Merry Muses of Caledonia*, compiled for a circle of Edinburgh clubmen, the Crochallan Fencibles. But it seems clear that he did not always, in his protestingly high-minded veins, mean what he said or say it well.

'The Vision' moves into a polite English with Coila's mandate to her rustic bard – his job is to write about love and to paint the manners of his class – and as he moves into English Burns grows more concerned to mind his own manners. If the poem is, as he intended it to be, a 'description of Kyle', it does not describe the lively place we find in the epistles. Once the introductory stanzas are over, Kyle yields the heroes and pictur-esque landscapes to which a man of feeling made it his business to respond.

> Thro' many a wild romantic grove,
> Near many a hermit-fancied cove
> (Fit haunts for Friendship or for Love
>   In musing mood)
> An agèd Judge, I saw him rove
>   Dispensing good.'

Burns is referring to Barskimming, seat of the judge Lord Glenlee, as he was to become. At different times this estate extracted the word 'romantic' or 'romance' from a group of people, a remarkable chorus, club or consensus composed of Robert Burns, David Hume and Henry Cockburn, while the nearby estate of Auchinleck, mentioned in an additional stanza contained in one version of the poem, was called 'romantic' by a son of the house, James Boswell.[5] Kyle counts, then, as a highly romantic vicinity. But it is far from obvious how much good the judge would have been able to dispense to the human race by behaving like a recluse: sensibility may be thought here to have perpetrated one of its characteristic false notes.

If love and poetry, and freedom and whisky, go together, as Burns thought, sensibility and hypocrisy do too, and he laid himself open to suspicions of insincerity. In her unfinished novel *Sanditon*, written in 1817, twenty years after the poet's death, Jane Austen conveys such suspicions very sharply. Her heroine converses, in Chapter 7, with Sir Edward, a foolish man of feeling for whom Burns was 'propelled', in art and life, by 'the sovereign impulses of illimitable ardour'. Charlotte won't have this sort of talk:

> 'I have read several of Burns' poems with great delight,' said Charlotte as soon as she had time to speak, 'but I am not poetic enough to separate a man's poetry entirely from his character; – and poor Burns' known irregularities, greatly interrupt my enjoyment of his lines. – I have difficulty in depending on the *truth* of his feelings as a lover. I have not faith in the *sincerity* of the affections of a man of his description. He felt and he wrote and he forgot.'

Burns's separations did not go unremarked by his early readers.

Another early reader was Byron, who was moved, by a private collection of Burns's letters, to speak, not of his separations, but of his mixtures or convergencies: 'What an antithetical mind! – tenderness, roughness – delicacy, coarseness – sentiment, sensuality – soaring and grovelling, dirt and deity – all mixed up in that one compound of inspired clay! It seems strange; a true voluptuary will never abandon his mind to the grossness of reality.'⁶ The case that may be made for the epistolary Burns has to decline Byron's unaccustomed (and perhaps class-conscious) primness on this occasion, and to insist that Burns's antithetical stuff may be better mixed up than sorted out.

Few people are likely to suspect that Burns's best behaviour was always hypocritical – always forced or affected: but his suspension between the life of a peasant and an admission to the gentry's tables, between radical sympathies and a late enlistment in the 'horse-leech' Excise, as he had previously referred to it in verse, gave rise to complexities and to falsities. With its devout father and stainless daughter, 'The Cotter's Saturday Night' is his best-behaved piece, and seems false to many readers now. One contemporary reader was willing to disparage it as being, in all its virtuous respectfulness, the least that could have been said about the cotter's Saturday nights which this woman remembered from her own childhood. She was the servant of Mrs Dunlop, to whom Burns wrote his most substantial letters and to whom his opinions were eventually to give offence, and she was suspicious of the poet. Ladies and gentlemen, she said, make much of this poem. But 'I dinna see how he could hae tauld it ony other way.'⁷ Burns himself may have reckoned that he was telling it the only way it could be told: but the poem is now felt to be vitiated by being told as to ladies and gentlemen. Scotland's poor did not expect to be described as jolly beggars, and we can take it that their manners embodied a response to the scrubbed doorsteps, clean living and deferential independence of mind which were expected of them by their betters, and depicted for them in literature. 'The Jolly Beggars' is an account of the poor with which they would have felt imperfectly at ease; 'The Cotter's Saturday Night' is an account of the poor which they may have been inclined to accept as no more than the truth.

Eight years before Jane Austen expressed her suspicions of Burns's sincerity, Francis Jeffrey passed judgment on his work in the *Edinburgh Review*.[8] For Jeffrey, a formidable arbiter of taste in the new Britain, Burns was an 'enamoured peasant', prone to the faults of a rustic vulgarity, and to faults of address in his dealings with the opposite sex, who was nonetheless 'entitled to the rank of a great and original genius'. His Scots was separate from, and not to be confused with, the 'barbarous dialects' of Yorkshire or Devon.

It is the language of a whole country – long an independent kingdom, and still separate in laws, character and manners. It is by no means peculiar to the vulgar; but is the common speech of the whole nation in early life – and, with many of its most exalted and accomplished individuals, throughout their whole existence; and, though it be true that, in later times, it has been, in some measure, laid aside by the more ambitious and aspiring of the present generation, it is still recollected, even by them, as the familiar language of their childhood, and of those who were the earliest objects of their love and veneration. It is connected, in their imagination, not only with that olden time which is uniformly conceived as more pure, lofty and simple than the present, but also with all the soft and bright colours of remembered childhood and domestic affection.

Jeffrey is writing here as a practitioner – in the line of Hartley and Archibald Alison – of the psychological aesthetic based on Associationism, in which value is derived from the establishment of connections, popularly known as the association of ideas, in early life. He is also writing as himself an aspiring, accomplished and exalted man, of whose speech it was said, in Scots, by his political opponent the Tory judge Lord Braxfield, that he had 'tint' (lost) his native tongue and found 'nae English'. None of this is any reason to doubt that what he says about the importance of Scots as the common speech of a whole nation in early life is true.

Jeffrey's friend, Henry Cockburn, lawyer and historian, pled in Scots: the language, as Lockhart affirmed in reporting his forensic eloquence, 'to whose music the ears around him had been taught to thrill in infancy'. But in 1844 Cockburn worried in his *Journal* that the language was dying: 'English has made no encroachment on me; yet, though I speak more Scotch than English throughout the day, and read Burns aloud, and recommend him, I cannot get even my own children to do more than pick up a queer word of him here and there. Scotch has ceased to be the vernacular language of the upper classes.'[9]

---

p. 17: Robert Burns's birthplace in Alloway. The living-room window of the 'auld clay biggin' built by the poet's father.
p. 18: The back of Burns Cottage, Alloway. Burns lived here until he was seven.
p. 19: Some Burns manuscripts and relics in Burns Cottage.
pp. 20 and 21: The Bachelors' Club, Tarbolton, Ayrshire, founded for the promotion of friendship and the improvement of the mind by Burns and other local young men in 1780.
p. 22: Unknown grave at Alloway's 'auld haunted kirk'.
p. 23: The grave of Robert Burns's father, William Burnes, at Alloway Kirk.
p. 24: Alloway Kirk, now derelict, half a mile from Burns Cottage.

The man who wrote this wrote it in English, and spoke English much of the time, while seeing himself as chiefly Scots-speaking. The man who worried about the death of Scots founded a school, Edinburgh Academy, which advertised for an English master who had to be fluent in pure English, and coached his daughter in the pronunciation of the South: please don't say 'Bawth'. Burns mattered to him in his dilemma, and would have spoken to him – as his own Scots speech did to susceptible juries – of childhood. His fear that Scots would die has proved greatly exaggerated. His forecast that the speech of most of his fellow-countrymen might have to be taught as a dead language in schools has yet to be fulfilled. It is spoken to this day, with Burns's childhood-intensive verse a factor in its survival, and we are entitled to hope that there will be something yet, in this respect, for a long time to come.

Also in 1844, in the *Journal* entry that followed these reflections, Cockburn recalled, from the turn of the century, a convivial, aristocratic Ayr. It was then 'filled with the families of gentlemen – from the country, from India, and from public service; and was a gay, card-playing, dancing, scandal-loving place'. Some of these aristocrats may well have spoken Scots, both privately and publicly (believing, in certain cases, perhaps, that their speech harked back to the Court Scots of a bygone age). But it was among such people, it was at the top, that the desertion of Scots would have been most forcibly apparent to Burns. By the poor, it had not been 'laid aside' in shame: 'the lower orders still speak Scotch,' noted Cockburn half a century later. But among the upper crust the 'encroachments' he describes were already well advanced. 'In splendid companies Scotch is not much heard,' reported Samuel Johnson in Edinburgh, on his way to the Western Isles.[10]

By 1844, according to Cockburn, 'the fashion of the Ayr world hath passed away'. Ayr, the unsurpassable, had been surpassed. The new era of swift communications, of railways, industry and commerce, threatened the native language by bringing English into Scotland, and had already brought about the death of Ayr. The growing metropolises of Glasgow and Edinburgh had, Cockburn felt, drained and left desolate such communities. The 'soul' of Ayr had gone with its gentry. The country seats were cold. 'The yellow gentlemen who now return from India take their idleness and their livers to Cheltenham or Bath' – or, as it was no longer proper to say, to Bawth. And yet there were plenty of people still left in Ayr, white people of the lower orders, who could be heard to speak a language which they were happy to recognise in the vernacular poetry of Burns.

'We twa hae paidled i' the burn' – the looking back over a life at the beginnings of that life, and the cherishing of the separate speech on which the recollection of those beginnings must depend, may have started in Burns's own lifetime, when Scots was to a large extent publicly discountenanced, and Mrs Dunlop's servant was among the first of many who have measured his poetry against their childhood. I am one of these people myself.

We grew up speaking the language in which we discovered that his most memorable pieces were written. At school, we memorised 'To a Mouse' and were made aware that artless rural maids should not be soiled. When Hugh MacDiarmid's modern Scots poem, 'Mars is braw in crammasy', was chalked up on the blackboard, we knew where we were, though there were those of us who must have wondered about that – for the same teachers who taught us 'To a Mouse' were capable of punishing a boy for speaking dialect, for saying 'shew' or 'shoo' instead of 'sew'. My grandmother said 'shew', said 'thole' for 'endure', said that so-and-so 'wrocht ower at Loanheid', just as Burns's farmer would have said: 'We twa hae wrocht ...'. Many of us acquired, as children, a reverence for his verse, which was quite compatible with a contempt for Burns Suppers and for the Burns mania and mart which rapidly arose in Scotland (at his execution in 1829, the murderer Burke knelt on a handkerchief which was given him and which carried a picture of the poet and some of his lines about misfortune), and for the idea that this should be the only poet in whom it was right to be interested.

At fifteen I cycled round Kyle and looked solemnly, one by one, at the farms in which he lived: I remember a stretch of dark grey wall, like the remnant of an old fortification, in the depths of a dark green countryside. Those who left the country to find work, and who took to saying 'worked' instead of 'wrocht' (the words, of course, are by origin the same), have held onto Burns as in later years they came to hold onto their childhood – for dear life. Such feelings are not, of course, confined to Scotland's absentees, and they have helped to perpetuate a worship of the poet which amounts to something decent and important – something yet, and something more than the tourist trade, with its Burns hankies and saucers, would lead one to think. The tall brown Victorian print of Burns, factor-like in his Mason's apron, which I remember dominating a living-room in a Midlothian miners' row was not there to issue any invitation to come to Scotland.

Burns's choice, for his most effective poems, of 'plain, braid Lallans', with its queer words, rather than English, his choice of a demotic idiom and a low style, has helped to ensure his permanence as a force in Scottish life, and it is not too much to say that the choice has been involved with the fate of Scotland itself, with its will to survive. At the same time, or so I have suggested, this choice was involved with another, which is less to be defined as a nationalistic preference for Scotland, as against England or Britain, than as the outcome of a hesitation between his ain folk, his Ayrshire folk, and the polite world of privilege and learning, where he appeared to applause but also on probation and on sufferance. Questions of class can be mistaken for questions of nationality. In its efforts to restore a separate Scotland – efforts which have promised very little in the way of a better life for those who live there – Scottish Nationalism has encouraged and exploited this mistake.

Another choice contemplated in his verse has also been suggested here: that between the company of men and the company of women. There are times, when we read him, when it can seem that the sexes were further apart than Scotland and England. Contrasting idioms and modes of address – a sentimental admiration of females, couched in the English of his best behaviour, as against the violence and leering of the separate and convivial male – tell the same story of a distance between the sexes. 'We twa' in Burns will seldom refer to a man and woman. And on occasion men and women can seem not only apart but at odds. They do not get on. They barely speak. This can be construed as one of the meanings of his masterpiece, 'Tam o' Shanter'.

In this poem, he has hung up his lyre and love has gone out of the window. What we have instead is the spectacle of a deeply sympathetic, and, as time was to tell, utterly representative, alcoholic voyeur. Tam's dame is at home, 'nursing her wrath to keep it warm' (I was very impressed, as a boy, by a glowering illustration which showed her doing this). Tam is out with his crony Souter Johnny, drowning his sorrows and (to be sure) flirting with the landlady. Then he has to climb on his horse and battle back drunk to endure his wife's wrath. He rides to Alloway Kirk, where a jolly coven is in damnable session, or so he hallucinates. Tam peeps at Nannie the witch in her 'scanty' shirt, at Satan with his bagpipes. At the hinder end of the poem comes the hinder end of Maggie the mare:

> Ae spring brought off her master hale,
> But left behind her ain gray tail:
> The carlin claught her by the rump,
> And left poor Maggie scarce a stump.

This teaches Tam the lesson that drink, with its visions of the cutty sark, may cost you your mare's tail – and your own: 'stump' would have carried for Burns a phallic sense or overtone, the 'reel of stumpie', for example, being a traditional name for sexual intercourse, and 'tail' could mean then what it can mean now. It is a lesson which alerts us to the presence in Hanoverian Scotland of a dangerous and delightful phantasmagoric alternative to sexuality and marriage: Scotland's national poem, with its peeping Tam and deep potations, whispers the overthrow of the sexual act. It tells of a Scotland in which sex and Scots could both be condemned, in which tongue and tail could both be tied, in which recourses and resistances had to be sought and imagined, and it predicts a Scotland in which its hero can, as I say, be thought a representative figure. In St Andrew's Square, Edinburgh, every Saturday night of my childhood, ten thousand Tams used to battle their way onto the last bus.

In considering this selection, I have made devoted use of James Kinsley's edition of the poems and songs. With its felicity of quotation from the wide range of poetry to which that of Burns attended, Kinsley's commentary must be accounted one of the most rewarding books to be written on the Scottish literature of the eighteenth century. The text of the poems is, with some minor adjustments, that of J. Logie Robertson's Oxford edition for the general reader, first published in 1904 and many times reissued. The text of three poems not given in the Robertson, 'Godly Girzie', 'Tibbie Fowler' and 'Lassie lie near me', is based on Kinsley's edition, and my reading of the dynamic 'Lass of Ecclefechan' has caused me to follow Kinsley by placing a comma, rather than Robertson's questionmark, after 'naething'. I am grateful to Christine Bold for providing a glossary and to William Graham for providing a key to the events of Burns's life.

Notes

1.   Thomas Crawford discusses 'The Jolly Beggars' in *Society and the Lyric* (1980, pp. 202–10). He expresses what could be called a romantic view of the poem, and takes issue with James Kinsley, who has held that ' "Love and Liberty" is not mythopoeic; its character is energetic and satiric realism'. For Crawford, it is both realism and myth: Burns sides with his beggars in such a way as to suggest that the energy affirmed in the poem is like the energy affirmed in Blake's aphorisms. 'The social character within the work is a profoundly critical comment on Burns's Scotland, which he was to explore again, quite seriously and indeed respectfully, in other poems such as "The Vision".'

2.   Ibid., pp. 6, 7. Crawford stresses that at this time the market for printed versions of popular songs was an all-British one. He compares (p. 11) some lines from an eighteenth-century song in polite English with a song in Scots by Burns ('Corn Rigs'), pointing out that the difference between them 'is more the difference between a high style and a colloquial style than between standard English and a regional dialect'. He goes on: 'It is not a matter of two poets employing different languages, but rather different registers or levels of usage within the same language.' The levels of usage perceived by Crawford may be understood with reference to differences of class within the society which spoke the language in question, and have been both determined and obscured by the regional variations in pronunciation and vocabulary which are perceived by many readers, so far as Scotland is concerned, as features of a second language. See also Graham Tulloch's *The Language of Walter Scott: A Study of his Scottish and Period Language* (1980, pp. 167–9 and 182), which explains how Scots started from 'the same base as Standard English' and developed phonologically along different lines, and tells how Scott set himself in his fiction, with Burns in mind, to keep alive the 'flame' of Scots speech and Scottish subjects.

3.   *The Poems and Songs of Robert Burns*, ed. James Kinsley, 3 vols, 1968, Vol. III, pp. 1069–74.

4.   *Preoccupations* by Seamus Heaney, 1980, pp. 116, 117.

5.   See Kinsley, Vol. III, pp. 1080, 1081, and *Cockburn's Millennium* (1975) by the present writer, p. 268.

6.   Quoted in Byron's *Letters and Journals*, 11 vols, ed. Leslie Marchand, Vol. I (1973), Introduction, p. 19.

7.   Kinsley, Vol. III, p. 1112.

8.   January 1809.

9.   See *Cockburn's Millennium*, p. 246, and Cockburn's *Journal* (1874), Vol. II, pp. 88–91.

10.   Johnson's report is quoted in Tulloch, p. 175.

THE POEMS

THE VISION

The sun had closed the winter day,
The curlers quat their roarin' play,
An' hunger'd maukin taen her way
    To kail-yards green,
While faithless snaws ilk step betray
    Where she has been.

The thresher's weary flingin'-tree
The lee-lang day had tirèd me;
And when the day had clos'd his e'e,
    Far i' the west,
Ben i' the spence, right pensivelie,
    I gaed to rest.

There lanely by the ingle-cheek
I sat and eyed the spewing reek,
That fill'd, wi' hoast-provoking smeek,
    The auld clay biggin';
An' heard the restless rattons squeak
    About the riggin'.

All in this mottie misty clime,
I backward mused on wasted time,
How I had spent my youthfu' prime,
    An' done nae-thing,
But stringin' blethers up in rhyme
    For fools to sing.

Had I to guid advice but harkit,
I might, by this, hae led a market,
Or strutted in a bank, and clarkit
    My cash-account:
While here, half-mad, half-fed, half-sarkit,
    Is a' th' amount.

I started, mutt'ring 'blockhead! coof!'
And heaved on high my waukit loof,
To swear by a' yon starry roof,
    Or some rash aith,
That I, henceforth, would be rhyme-proof
    Till my last breath –

When click! the string the snick did draw;
An' jee! the door gaed to the wa';
And by my ingle-lowe I saw,
      Now bleezin' bright,
A tight outlandish hizzie, braw,
      Come full in sight.

Ye need na doubt I held my whisht;
The infant aith, half-form'd, was crusht;
I glowr'd as eerie 's I'd been dusht
      In some wild glen;
When sweet, like modest worth, she blusht,
      An' steppèd ben.

Green, slender, leaf-clad holly-boughs
Were twisted, gracefu', round her brows;
I took her for some Scottish Muse
      By that same token;
And come to stop these reckless vows,
      Would soon been broken.

A hare-brain'd, sentimental trace,
Was strongly markèd in her face;
A wildly-witty rustic grace
      Shone full upon her;
Her eye, ev'n turn'd on empty space,
      Beam'd keen with honour.

Down flow'd her robe, a tartan sheen,
Till half a leg was scrimply seen;
An' such a leg! my bonnie Jean
      Could only peer it;
Sae straught, sae taper, tight, and clean,
      Nane else came near it.

Her mantle large, of greenish hue,
My gazing wonder chiefly drew;
Deep lights and shades, bold-mingling, threw
      A lustre grand;
And seem'd to my astonish'd view
      A well-known land.

Here rivers in the sea were lost;
There mountains to the skies were tost:
Here tumbling billows mark'd the coast
      With surging foam;
There, distant shone Art's lofty boast,
      The lordly dome.

Here Doon pour'd down his far-fetch'd floods;
There well-fed Irwine stately thuds;
Auld hermit Ayr staw thro' his woods,
    On to the shore;
And many a lesser torrent scuds,
    With seeming roar.

Low in a sandy valley spread,
An ancient borough rear'd her head;
Still, as in Scottish story read,
    She boasts a race,
To ev'ry nobler virtue bred,
    And polish'd grace.

By stately tower or palace fair,
Or ruins pendent in the air,
Bold stems of heroes, here and there,
    I could discern;
Some seem'd to muse, some seem'd to dare,
    With feature stern.

My heart did glowing transport feel,
To see a race heroic wheel,
And brandish round, the deep-dyed steel
    In sturdy blows;
While back-recoiling seem'd to reel
    Their Suthron foes.

His Country's Saviour, mark him well!
Bold Richardton's heroic swell;
The Chief - on Sark who glorious fell,
    In high command;
And he whom ruthless fates expel
    His native land.

There, where a sceptred Pictish shade
Stalk'd round his ashes lowly laid,
I mark'd a martial race, pourtray'd
    In colours strong;
Bold, soldier-featur'd, undismay'd
    They strode along.

Thro' many a wild romantic grove,
Near many a hermit-fancied cove
(Fit haunts for Friendship or for Love
    In musing mood)
An agèd Judge, I saw him rove
    Dispensing good.

With deep-struck reverential awe
The learned Sire and Son I saw;
To Nature's God and Nature's law
      They gave their lore;
This, all its source and end to draw,
      That, to adore.

Brydon's brave ward I well could spy,
Beneath old Scotia's smiling eye;
Who call'd on Fame, low standing by,
      To hand him on,
Where many a patriot name on high,
      And hero shone.

DUAN SECOND

With musing-deep astonish'd stare,
I view'd the heavenly-seeming Fair;
A whisp'ring throb did witness bear
      Of kindred sweet,
When with an elder Sister's air
      She did me greet.

'All hail! my own inspired bard!
In me thy native Muse regard!
Nor longer mourn thy fate is hard,
      Thus poorly low;
I come to give thee such reward
      As we bestow.

'Know the great Genius of this land
Has many a light aërial band,
Who, all beneath his high command,
      Harmoniously,
As arts or arms they understand,
      Their labours ply.

'They Scotia's race among them share:
Some fire the soldier on to dare;
Some rouse the patriot up to bare
      Corruption's heart:
Some teach the bard, a darling care,
      The tuneful art.

''Mong swelling floods of reeking gore,
They, ardent, kindling spirits pour;
Or, 'mid the venal senate's roar,
      They, sightless, stand,
To mend the honest patriot lore,
      And grace the hand.

'And when the bard, or hoary sage,
Charm or instruct the future age,
They bind the wild poetic rage
      In energy,
Or point the inconclusive page
      Full on the eye.

'Hence Fullarton, the brave and young;
Hence Dempster's zeal-inspirèd tongue;
Hence sweet harmonious Beattie sung
      His Minstrel lays,
Or tore, with noble ardour stung,
      The sceptic's bays.

'To lower orders are assign'd
The humbler ranks of human-kind,
The rustic bard, the lab'ring hind,
      The artisan;
All choose, as various they're inclin'd,
      The various man.

'When yellow waves the heavy grain,
The threat'ning storm some strongly rein;
Some teach to meliorate the plain
      With tillage-skill;
And some instruct the shepherd-train,
      Blythe o'er the hill.

'Some hint the lover's harmless wile;
Some grace the maiden's artless smile;
Some soothe the lab'rer's weary toil
      For humble gains,
And make his cottage-scenes beguile
      His cares and pains.

'Some, bounded to a district-space,
Explore at large man's infant race,
To mark the embryotic trace
      Of rustic bard;
And careful note each op'ning grace,
      A guide and guard.

'Of these am I – Coila my name;
And this district as mine I claim,
Where once the Campbells, chiefs of fame,
  Held ruling pow'r:
I mark'd thy embryo-tuneful flame,
  Thy natal hour.

'With future hope I oft would gaze,
Fond, on thy little early ways,
Thy rudely-caroll'd, chiming phrase,
  In uncouth rhymes, –
Fired at the simple artless lays
  Of other times.

'I saw thee seek the sounding shore,
Delighted with the dashing roar;
Or when the North his fleecy store
  Drove thro' the sky,
I saw grim Nature's visage hoar
  Struck thy young eye.

'Or when the deep green-mantled Earth
Warm-cherish'd ev'ry flow'ret's birth,
And joy and music pouring forth
  In ev'ry grove,
I saw thee eye the gen'ral mirth
  With boundless love.

'When ripen'd fields and azure skies
Call'd forth the reapers' rustling noise,
I saw thee leave their ev'ning joys,
  And lonely stalk,
To vent thy bosom's swelling rise
  In pensive walk.

'When youthful love, warm-blushing strong,
Keen-shivering shot thy nerves along,
Those accents, grateful to thy tongue,
  Th' adorèd Name,
I taught thee how to pour in song,
  To soothe thy flame.

'I saw thy pulse's maddening play
Wild send thee pleasure's devious way,
Misled by fancy's meteor ray,
  By passion driven;
But yet the light that led astray
  Was light from Heaven.

'I taught thy manners-painting strains,
The loves, the ways of simple swains,
Till now, o'er all my wide domains
      Thy fame extends;
And some, the pride of Coila's plains,
      Become thy friends.

'Thou canst not learn, nor can I show,
To paint with Thomson's landscape-glow;
Or wake the bosom-melting throe
      With Shenstone's art;
Or pour with Gray the moving flow
      Warm on the heart.

'Yet all beneath th' unrivall'd rose
The lowly daisy sweetly blows;
Tho' large the forest's monarch throws
      His army shade,
Yet green the juicy hawthorn grows
      Adown the glade.

'Then never murmur nor repine;
Strive in thy humble sphere to shine;
And trust me, not Potosi's mine,
      Nor king's regard,
Can give a bliss o'ermatching thine,
      A rustic Bard.

'To give my counsels all in one,
Thy tuneful flame still careful fan;
Preserve the dignity of Man,
      With Soul erect;
And trust the Universal Plan
      Will all protect.

'And wear thou this': She solemn said,
And bound the holly round my head:
The polish'd leaves and berries red
      Did rustling play;
And, like a passing thought, she fled
      In light away.

TO WILLIAM SIMPSON

I gat your letter, winsome Willie;
Wi' gratefu' heart I thank you brawlie;
Tho' I maun say't, I wad be silly,
    An' unco vain,
Should I believe, my coaxin' billie,
    Your flatterin' strain.

But I'se believe ye kindly meant it:
I sud be laith to think ye hinted
Ironic satire, sidelins sklented
    On my poor Musie;
Tho' in sic phraisin' terms ye've penn'd it,
    I scarce excuse ye.

My senses wad be in a creel,
Should I but dare a hope to speel,
Wi' Allan, or wi' Gilbertfield,
    The braes o' fame;
Or Fergusson, the writer-chiel,
    A deathless name.

(O Fergusson! thy glorious parts
Ill suited law's dry, musty arts!
My curse upon your whunstane hearts,
    Ye E'nbrugh gentry!
The tythe o' what ye waste at cartes
    Wad stow'd his pantry!)

Yet when a tale comes i' my head,
Or lasses gie my heart a screed,
As whiles they're like to be my dead,
    (O sad disease!)
I kittle up my rustic reed;
    It gies me ease.

Auld Coila, now, may fidge fu' fain,
She's gotten poets o' her ain,
Chiels wha their chanters winna hain,
    But tune their lays,
Till echoes a' resound again
    Her weel-sung praise.

Nae poet thought her worth his while,
To set her name in measur'd style;
She lay like some unkenn'd-of isle,
      Beside New Holland,
Or where wild-meeting oceans boil
      Besouth Magellan.

Ramsay an' famous Fergusson
Gied Forth an' Tay a lift aboon;
Yarrow an' Tweed, to mony a tune,
      Owre Scotland rings,
While Irwin, Lugar, Ayr, an' Doon,
      Naebody sings.

Th' Ilissus, Tiber, Thames, an' Seine,
Glide sweet in mony a tunefu' line;
But, Willie, set your fit to mine,
      An' cock your crest,
We'll gar our streams an' burnies shine
      Up wi' the best.

We'll sing auld Coila's plains an' fells,
Her moors red-brown wi' heather bells,
Her banks an' braes, her dens an' dells,
      Where glorious Wallace
Aft bure the gree, as story tells,
      Frae Southron billies.

At Wallace' name, what Scottish blood
But boils up in a spring-tide flood!
Oft have our fearless fathers strode
      By Wallace' side,
Still pressing onward, red-wat-shod,
      Or glorious died.

O, sweet are Coila's haughs an' woods,
When lintwhites chant amang the buds,
And jinkin' hares, in amorous whids,
      Their loves enjoy,
While thro' the braes the cushat croods
      Wi' wailfu' cry!

Ev'n winter bleak has charms to me
When winds rave thro' the naked tree;
Or frosts on hills of Ochiltree
      Are hoary gray;
Or blinding drifts wild-furious flee,
      Dark'ning the day!

O Nature! a' thy shews an' forms
To feeling, pensive hearts hae charms!
Whether the summer kindly warms,
　　　Wi' life an' light,
Or winter howls, in gusty storms,
　　　The lang, dark night!

The Muse, nae poet ever fand her,
Till by himsel he learn'd to wander
Adown some trottin' burn's meander,
　　　An' no think lang;
O sweet, to stray an' pensive ponder
　　　A heart-felt sang!

The warly race may drudge an' drive,
Hog-shouther, jundie, stretch, an' strive;
Let me fair Nature's face descrive,
　　　And I, wi' pleasure,
Shall let the busy, grumbling hive
　　　Bum owre their treasure.

Fareweel, 'my rhyme-composing brither!'
We've been owre lang unkenn'd to ither:
Now let us lay our heads thegither,
　　　In love fraternal;
May Envy wallop in a tether,
　　　Black fiend infernal!

While Highlandmen hate tolls an' taxes;
While moorlan' herds like guid fat braxies;
While Terra Firma, on her axis,
　　　Diurnal turns,
Count on a friend, in faith an' practice,
　　　In Robert Burns.

(continued on p. 49)

POSTCRIPT

My memory's no worth a preen;
I had amaist forgotten clean,
Ye bade me write you what they mean
   By this New-Light,
'Bout which our herds sae aft have been
   Maist like to fight.

In days when mankind were but callans
At grammar, logic, an' sic talents,
They took nae pains their speech to balance,
   Or rules to gie,
But spak their thoughts in plain, braid Lallans,
   Like you or me.

In thae auld times, they thought the moon,
Just like a sark, or pair o' shoon,
Wore by degrees, till her last roon,
   Gaed past their viewin',
An' shortly after she was done,
   They gat a new one.

This past for certain, undisputed;
It ne'er cam i' their heads to doubt it,
Till chiels gat up an' wad confute it,
   An' ca'd it wrang;
An' muckle din there was about it,
   Baith loud an' lang.

Some herds, weel learn'd upo' the beuk,
Wad threap auld folk the thing misteuk;
For 'twas the auld moon turn'd a neuk,
   An' out o' sight,
An' backlins-comin, to the leuk,
   She grew mair bright.

This was deny'd, it was affirm'd;
The herds an' hissels were alarm'd:
The rev'rend gray-beards rav'd an' storm'd,
   That beardless laddies
Should think they better were inform'd
   Than their auld daddies.

Frae less to mair it gaed to sticks;
Frae words an' aiths to clours an' nicks;
An' mony a fallow gat his licks,
    Wi' hearty crunt;
An' some, to learn them for their tricks,
    Were hang'd an' brunt.

This game was play'd in mony lands,
An' auld-light caddies bure sic hands,
That, faith, the youngsters took the sands
    Wi' nimble shanks;
The lairds forbad, by strict commands,
    Sic bluidy pranks.

But new-light herds gat sic a cowe,
Folk thought them ruin'd stick-an-stowe,
Till now amaist on ev'ry knowe
    Ye'll find ane plac'd;
An' some, their new-light fair avow,
    Just quite barefac'd.

Nae doubt the auld-light flocks are bleatin';
Their zealous herds are vex'd an' sweatin';
Mysel, I've even seen them greetin'
    Wi' girnin spite,
To hear the moon sae sadly lied on
    By word an' write.

But shortly they will cowe the louns!
Some auld-light herds in neibor-touns
Are mind't, in things they ca' balloons,
    To take a flight,
An' stay ae month amang the moons,
    An' see them right.

Guid observation they will gie them;
An' when the auld moon 's gaun to lea'e them,
The hindmost shaird, they'll fetch it wi' them,
    Just i' their pouch,
An' when the new-light billies see them,
    I think they'll crouch!

Sae, ye observe that a' this clatter
Is naething but a 'moonshine matter';
But tho' dull-prose folk Latin splatter
    In logic tulzie,
I hope we bardies ken some better
    Than mind sic brulzie.

TO JAMES SMITH

Dear Smith, the sleeest pawkie thief
That e'er attempted stealth or rief,
Ye surely hae some warlock-breef
   Owre human hearts;
For ne'er a bosom yet was prief
   Against your arts.

For me, I swear by sun an' moon,
And ev'ry star that blinks aboon,
Ye've cost me twenty pair o' shoon
   Just gaun to see you;
And ev'ry ither pair that's done,
   Mair taen I'm wi' you.

That auld capricious carlin', Nature,
To mak amends for scrimpit stature,
She's turn'd you aff, a human creature
   On her first plan,
And in her freaks, on ev'ry feature,
   She's wrote 'The Man.'

Just now I've taen the fit o' rhyme,
My barmie noddle's working prime,
My fancie yerkit up sublime
   Wi' hasty summon:
Hae ye a leisure-moment's time
   To hear what's comin'?

Some rhyme a neebor's name to lash;
Some rhyme (vain thought!) for needfu' cash;
Some rhyme to court the country clash,
   An' raise a din;
For me, an aim I never fash;
   I rhyme for fun.

The star that rules my luckless lot,
Has fated me the russet coat,
An' damn'd my fortune to the groat;
   But, in requit,
Has blest me with a random shot
   O' country wit.

This while my notion 's taen a sklent,
To try my fate in guid, black prent;
But still the mair I'm that way bent,
   Something cries 'Hoolie!
I red you, honest man, tak tent!
   Ye'll shaw your folly.

'There's ither poets, much your betters,
Far seen in Greek, deep men o' letters,
Hae thought they had ensured their debtors
   A' future ages;
Now moths deform in shapeless tatters
   Their unknown pages.'

Then fareweel hopes o' laurel-boughs,
To garland my poetic brows!
Henceforth I'll rove where busy ploughs
   Are whistling thrang,
An' teach the lanely heights an' howes
   My rustic sang.

I'll wander on, wi' tentless heed
How never-halting moments speed,
Till fate shall snap the brittle thread;
   Then, all unknown,
I'll lay me with th' inglorious dead,
   Forgot and gone!

But why o' death begin a tale?
Just now we're living sound an' hale;
Then top and maintop crowd the sail,
   Heave Care o'er side!
And large, before Enjoyment's gale,
   Let's tak the tide.

This life, sae far's I understand,
Is a' enchanted fairy-land,
Where pleasure is the magic wand,
   That, wielded right,
Maks hours like minutes, hand in hand,
   Dance by fu' light.

The magic wand then let us wield:
For, ance that five-an'-forty's speel'd,
See, crazy, weary, joyless Eild,
   Wi' wrinkled face,
Comes hoastin', hirplin' owre the field,
   Wi' creepin' pace.

When ance life's day draws near the gloamin',
Then fareweel vacant careless roamin';
An' fareweel cheerfu' tankards foamin',
    An' social noise;
An' fareweel dear deluding woman,
    The joy of joys!

O life, how pleasant is thy morning,
Young Fancy's rays the hills adorning!
Cold-pausing Caution's lesson scorning,
    We frisk away,
Like schoolboys, at th' expected warning,
    To joy and play.

We wander there, we wander here,
We eye the rose upon the brier,
Unmindful that the thorn is near,
    Among the leaves:
And tho' the puny wound appear,
    Short while it grieves.

Some, lucky, find a flow'ry spot,
For which they never toil'd nor swat;
They drink the sweet and eat the fat,
    But care or pain;
And, haply, eye the barren hut
    With high disdain.

With steady aim, some Fortune chase;
Keen hope does ev'ry sinew brace;
Thro' fair, thro' foul, they urge the race,
    And seize the prey;
Then cannie, in some cozie place,
    They close the day.

And others, like your humble servan',
Poor wights! nae rules nor roads observin',
To right or left, eternal swervin',
    They zig-zag on;
Till curst with age, obscure an' starvin',
    They often groan.

Alas! what bitter toil an' straining –
But truce wi' peevish, poor complaining!
Is Fortune's fickle Luna waning?
    E'en let her gang!
Beneath what light she has remaining,
    Let's sing our sang.

My pen I here fling to the door,
And kneel 'Ye Pow'rs!' and warm implore,
'Tho' I should wander Terra o'er,
          In all her climes,
Grant me but this, I ask no more,
          Aye rowth o' rhymes.

'Gie dreeping roasts to country lairds,
Till icicles hing frae their beards;
Gie fine braw claes to fine life-guards,
          And maids of honour;
And yill an' whisky gie to cairds,
          Until they sconner.

'A title, Dempster merits it;
A garter gie to Willie Pitt;
Gie wealth to some be-ledger'd cit,
          In cent per cent;
But gie me real, sterling wit,
          And I'm content.

'While ye are pleased to keep me hale,
I'll sit down o'er my scanty meal,
Be't water-brose, or muslin-kail,
          Wi' cheerfu' face,
As lang's the Muses dinna fail
          To say the grace.'

An anxious e'e I never throws
Behint my lug, or by my nose;
I jouk beneath misfortune's blows
          As weel's I may;
Sworn foe to sorrow, care, and prose,
          I rhyme away.

O ye douce folk, that live by rule,
Grave, tideless-blooded, calm, and cool,
Compar'd wi' you – O fool! fool! fool!
          How much unlike!
Your hearts are just a standing pool,
          Your lives a dyke!

Nae hare-brain'd sentimental traces,
In your unletter'd, nameless faces!
In arioso trills and graces
          Ye never stray,
But gravissimo, solemn basses,
          Ye hum away.

Ye are sae grave, nae doubt ye're wise;
Nae ferly tho' ye do despise
The hairum-scairum, ram-stam boys,
    The rattlin' squad:
I see you upward cast your eyes –
    Ye ken the road.

Whilst I – but I shall haud me there –
Wi' you I'll scarce gang ony where –
Then, Jamie, I shall say nae mair,
    But quat my sang,
Content with You to mak a pair,
    Where'er I gang.

EPISTLE TO MAJOR LOGAN

Hail, thairm-inspirin', rattlin' Willie!
Though fortune's road be rough an' hilly
To every fiddling, rhyming billie,
    We never heed,
But take it like the unback'd filly,
    Proud o' her speed.

When idly govin' whyles we saunter,
Yirr, fancy barks, awa' we canter
Uphill, down brae, till some mishanter,
    Some black bog-hole,
Arrests us, then the scathe an' banter
    We're forced to thole.

Hale be your heart! hale be your fiddle!
Lang may your elbuck jink and diddle,
To cheer you through the weary widdle
    O' this wild warl',
Until you on a crummock driddle
    A gray-hair'd carl.

Come wealth, come poortith, late or soon,
Heaven send your heart-strings aye in tune,
And screw your temper-pins aboon,
    A fifth or mair,
The melancholious lazy croon,
    O' cankrie care.

May still your life from day to day
Nae 'lente largo' in the play,
But 'allegretto forte' gay
          Harmonious flow,
A sweeping, kindling, bauld strathspey –
          Encore! Bravo!

A blessing on the cheery gang
Wha dearly like a jig or sang,
An' never think o' right an' wrang
          By square an' rule,
But as the clegs o' feeling stang
          Are wise or fool.

My hand-waled curse keep hard in chase
The harpy, hoodock, purse-proud race,
Wha count on poortith as disgrace –
          Their tuneless hearts!
May fire-side discords jar a base
          To a' their parts!

But come, your hand, my careless brither,
I' th' ither warl' if there's anither,
An' that there is I've little swither
          About the matter;
We cheek for chow shall jog thegither,
          I'se ne'er bid better.

We've faults and failings – granted clearly,
We're frail backsliding mortals merely,
Eve's bonnie squad priests wyte them sheerly
          For our grand fa';
But still, but still, I like them dearly –
          God bless them a'!

Ochone for poor Castalian drinkers,
When they fa' foul o' earthly jinkers,
The witching cursed delicious blinkers
          Hae put me hyte,
And gart me weet my waukrife winkers,
          Wi' girnin' spite.

But by yon moon! – and that's high swearin' –
An' every star within my hearin'!
An' by her een wha was a dear ane!
          I'll ne'er forget;
I hope to gie the jads a clearin'
          In fair play yet.

My loss I mourn, but not repent it,
I'll seek my pursie where I tint it;
Ance to the Indies I were wonted,
    Some cantraip hour,
By some sweet elf I'll yet be dinted,
    Then *vive l'amour!*

Faites mes baissemains respectueuse
To sentimental sister Susie,
An' honest Lucky; no to roose you,
    Ye may be proud
That sic a couple Fate allows ye
    To grace your blood.

Nae mair at present can I measure,
An' trowth my rhymin' ware's nae treasure;
But when in Ayr, some half hour's leisure,
    Be't light, be't dark,
Sir Bard will do himself the pleasure
    To call at Park.

LETTER TO JAMES TENNANT, GLENCONNER

Auld comrade dear and brither sinner,
How's a' the folk about Glenconner?
How do you this blae eastlin wind,
That's like to blaw a body blind?
For me, my faculties are frozen,
My dearest member nearly dozen'd.
I've sent you here by Johnie Simson,
Twa sage philosophers to glimpse on;
Smith, wi' his sympathetic feeling,
An' Reid, to common sense appealing.
Philosophers have fought an' wrangled,
An' meikle Greek an' Latin mangled,
Till wi' their logic-jargon tir'd,
An' in the depth of Science mir'd,
To common sense they now appeal,
What wives an' wabsters see an' feel.
But, hark ye, friend, I charge you strictly,
Peruse them, an' return them quickly;
For now I'm grown sae cursèd douce,
I pray an' ponder but the house;

My shins, my lane, I there sit roastin',
Perusing Bunyan, Brown, an' Boston;
Till by an' by, if I haud on,
I'll grunt a real Gospel-groan:
Already I begin to try it,
To cast my een up like a pyet,
When by the gun she tumbles o'er,
Flutt'ring an' gaspin' in her gore:
Sae shortly you shall see me bright,
A burning an' a shining light.

    My heart-warm love to guid auld Glen,
The ace an' wale of honest men:
When bending down wi' auld grey hairs,
Beneath the load of years and cares,
May He who made him still support him,
An' views beyond the grave comfort him.
His worthy fam'ly far and near,
God bless them a' wi' grace and gear!

    My auld school-fellow, Preacher Willie,
The manly tar, my mason billie,
An' Auchenbay, I wish him joy;
If he's a parent, lass or boy,
May he be dad, and Meg the mither
Just five-and-forty years thegither!
An' no forgetting wabster Charlie,
I'm tauld he offers very fairly.
An' Lord, remember singing Sannock,
Wi' hale-breeks, saxpence, an' a bannock.
An' next, my auld acquaintance, Nancy,
Since she is fitted to her fancy,
An' her kind stars hae airted till her
A good chiel wi' a pickle siller.
My kindest, best respects I sen' it,
To cousin Kate an' sister Janet;
Tell them frae me, wi' chiels be cautious,
For, faith, they'll aiblins fin' them fashious:
To grant a heart is fairly civil,
But to grant a maidenhead's the devil.
An' lastly, Jamie, for yoursel,
May guardian angels tak a spell,
An' steer you seven miles south o' hell:
But first, before you see heav'n's glory,
May ye get mony a merry story,
Mony a laugh, and mony a drink,
An' aye enough o' needfu' clink.

    Now fare ye weel, an' joy be wi' you!
For my sake, this I beg it o' you,
Assist poor Simson a' ye can,

Ye'll fin' him just an honest man;
Sae I conclude and quat my chanter,
Yours, saint or sinner,
ROB THE RANTER.

EPISTLE TO HUGH PARKER

In this strange land, this uncouth clime,
A land unknown to prose or rhyme;
Where words ne'er crost the Muse's heckles,
Nor limpit in poetic shackles;
A land that prose did never view it,
Except when drunk he stacher't through it;
Here, ambush'd by the chimla cheek,
Hid in an atmosphere of reek,
I hear a wheel thrum i' the neuk,
I hear it - for in vain I leuk.
The red peat gleams, a fiery kernel,
Enhuskèd by a fog infernal;
Here, for my wonted rhyming raptures,
I sit and count my sins by chapters;
For life and spunk like ither Christians, –
I'm dwindled down to mere existence,
Wi' nae converse but Gallowa' bodies,
Wi' nae kend face but Jenny Geddes.
Jenny, my Pegasean pride!
Dowie she saunters down Nithside,
And ay a westlin leuk she throws,
While tears hap o'er her auld brown nose!
Was it for this, wi' canny care,
Thou bure the Bard through many a shire?
At howes or hillocks never stumbled,
And late or early never grumbled?
O, had I power like inclination,
I'd heeze thee up a constellation,
To canter with the Sagitarre,
Or loup the ecliptic like a bar;
Or turn the pole like any arrow;
Or, when auld Phoebus bids good-morrow,
Down the zodiac urge the race,
And cast dirt on his godship's face;
For I could lay my bread and kail
He'd ne'er cast saut upo' thy tail.
Wi' a' this care and a' this grief,
And sma', sma' prospect of relief,

And nought but peat reek i' my head,
How can I write what ye can read?
Tarbolton, twenty-fourth o' June,
Ye'll find me in a better tune;
But till we meet and weet our whistle,
Tak this excuse for nae epistle.

HOLY WILLIE'S PRAYER

O Thou, wha in the Heavens dost dwell,
Wha, as it pleases best thysel',
Sends ane to heaven and ten to hell,
   A' for thy glory,
And no for ony guid or ill
    They've done afore thee!

I bless and praise thy matchless might,
Whan thousands thou hast left in night,
That I am here afore thy sight,
   For gifts an' grace
A burnin' an' a shinin' light,
    To a' this place.

What was I, or my generation,
That I should get sic exaltation?
I, wha deserve most just damnation,
   For broken laws,
Sax thousand years 'fore my creation,
    Thro' Adam's cause.

When frae my mither's womb I fell,
Thou might hae plungèd me in hell,
To gnash my gums, to weep and wail,
   In burnin' lakes,
Where damnèd devils roar and yell,
    Chain'd to their stakes;

Yet I am here a chosen sample,
To show thy grace is great and ample;
I'm here a pillar in thy temple,
   Strong as a rock,
A guide, a buckler, an example
    To a' thy flock.

O Lord, thou kens what zeal I bear,
When drinkers drink, and swearers swear,
And singin' there and dancin' here,
      Wi' great an' sma':
For I am keepit by thy fear
      Free frae them a'.

But yet, O Lord! confess I must
At times I'm fash'd wi' fleshly lust;
An' sometimes too, in warldly trust,
      Vile self gets in;
But thou remembers we are dust,
      Defil'd in sin.

O Lord! yestreen, thou kens, wi' Meg –
Thy pardon I sincerely beg;
O! may't ne'er be a livin' plague
      To my dishonour,
An' I'll ne'er lift a lawless leg
      Again upon her.

Besides I farther maun allow,
Wi' Lizzie's lass, three times I trow –
But, Lord, that Friday I was fou,
      When I cam near her,
Or else thou kens thy servant true
      Wad never steer her.

May be thou lets this fleshly thorn
Beset thy servant e'en and morn
Lest he owre high and proud should turn,
      That he's sae gifted;
If sae, thy hand maun e'en be borne,
      Until thou lift it.

Lord, bless thy chosen in this place,
For here thou hast a chosen race;
But God confound their stubborn face,
      And blast their name,
Wha bring thy elders to disgrace
      An' public shame.

Lord, mind Gawn Hamilton's deserts,
He drinks, an' swears, an' plays at cartes,
Yet has sae mony takin' arts
      Wi' grit an' sma',
Frae God's ain priest the people's hearts
      He steals awa'.

An' when we chasten'd him therefor,
Thou kens how he bred sic a splore
As set the warld in a roar
   O' laughin' at us;
Curse thou his basket and his store,
   Kail and potatoes.

Lord, hear my earnest cry an' pray'r,
Against that presbyt'ry o' Ayr;
Thy strong right hand, Lord, make it bare
   Upo' their heads;
Lord, weigh it down, and dinna spare,
   For their misdeeds.

O Lord my God, that glib-tongu'd Aiken,
My very heart and soul are quakin',
To think how we stood sweatin', shakin',
   An' piss'd wi' dread,
While he, wi' hingin' lips and snakin',
   Held up his head.

Lord, in the day of vengeance try him;
Lord, visit them wha did employ him,
And pass not in thy mercy by them,
   Nor hear their pray'r:
But, for thy people's sake, destroy them,
   And dinna spare.

But, Lord, remember me and mine
Wi' mercies temp'ral and divine,
That I for gear and grace may shine
   Excell'd by nane,
And a' the glory shall be thine,
   Amen, Amen!

GODLY GIRZIE

The night it was a haly night,
 The day had been a haly day;
Kilmarnock gleam'd wi' candle light,
 As Girzie hameward took her way.
A man o' sin, ill may he thrive!
 And never haly-meeting see!
Wi' godly Girzie met belyve,
 Amang the Craigie hills sae hie.

The chiel was wight, the chiel was stark,
  He wad na wait to chap nor ca',
And she was faint wi' haly wark,
  She had na pith to say him na.
But ay she glowr'd up to the moon,
  And ay she sigh'd most piouslie;
'I trust my heart's in heaven aboon,
  Whare'er your sinfu' pintle be.'

ADDRESS TO THE DEIL

O thou! whatever title suit thee,
Auld Hornie, Satan, Nick, or Clootie,
Wha in yon cavern grim an' sootie,
      Clos'd under hatches,
Spairges about the brunstane cootie,
      To scaud poor wretches!

Hear me, auld Hangie, for a wee,
An' let poor damnèd bodies be;
I'm sure sma' pleasure it can gie,
      Ev'n to a deil,
To skelp an' scaud poor dogs like me,
      An' hear us squeal!

Great is thy pow'r, an' great thy fame;
Far kenn'd an' noted is thy name;
An', tho' yon lowin heugh's thy hame,
      Thou travels far;
An' faith! thou's neither lag nor lame,
      Nor blate nor scaur.

Whyles rangin' like a roarin' lion
For prey, a' holes an' corners tryin';
Whyles on the strong-wing'd tempest flyin',
      Tirlin' the kirks;
Whyles, in the human bosom pryin',
      Unseen thou lurks.

I've heard my reverend grannie say,
In lanely glens ye like to stray;
Or, where auld ruin'd castles gray
      Nod to the moon,
Ye fright the nightly wand'rer's way,
      Wi' eldritch croon.

When twilight did my grannie summon
To say her pray'rs, douce, honest woman!
Aft yont the dyke she's heard you bummin',
  Wi' eerie drone;
Or, rustlin', thro' the boortrees comin',
  Wi' heavy groan.

Ae dreary windy winter night
The stars shot down wi' sklentin' light,
Wi' you mysel I gat a fright
  Ayont the lough;
Ye like a rash-buss stood in sight
  Wi' waving sough.

The cudgel in my nieve did shake,
Each bristled hair stood like a stake,
When wi' an eldritch stoor 'quaick, quaick,'
  Amang the springs,
Awa ye squatter'd like a drake
  On whistlin' wings.

Let warlocks grim an' wither'd hags
Tell how wi' you on ragweed nags
They skim the muirs, an' dizzy crags
  Wi' wicked speed;
And in kirk-yards renew their leagues
  Owre howkit dead.

(continued on p. 73)

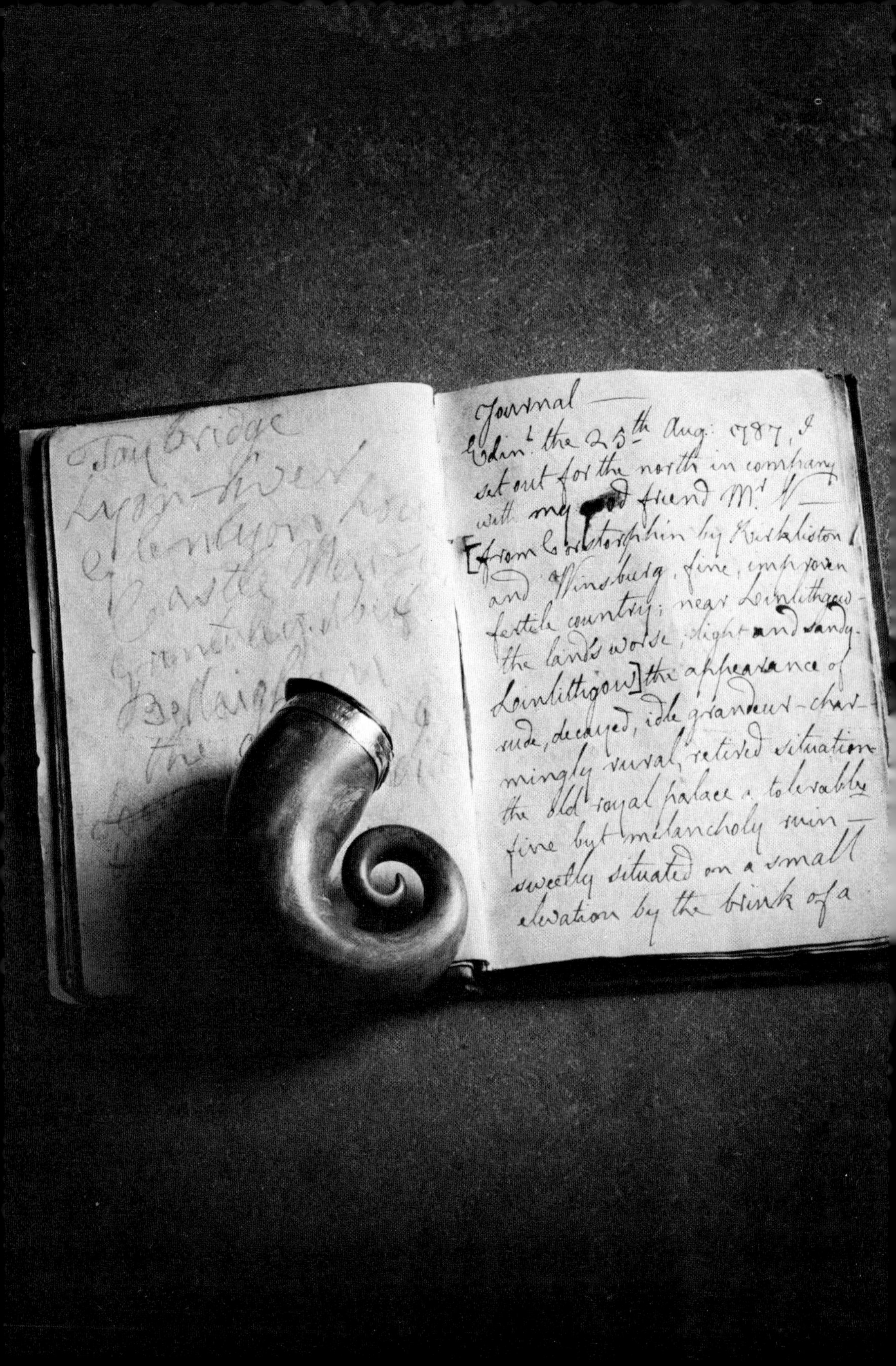

Tay bridge
Lyon house
Glenlyon house
Castle Menzies
Dunkeld...
Blair...

Right page:
Journal —
Edin.̲ the 25.th Aug:ͭ 787, I
set out for the north in company
with my good friend M.ͬ ⁁ —
[from Corstorphin by Kirkliston
and Winsburg, fine, improven
fertile country; near Linlithgow
the lands worse, light and sandy.
Linlithgow] the appearance of
rude, decayed, idle grandeur — char-
mingly rural, retired situation
the old royal palace a tolerable
fine but melancholy ruin
sweetly situated on a small
elevation by the brink of a

Auld lang fyne.
Methinks around us on each bough
A thousand Cupids play,
Whilst through the groves I walk with you,
Each object makes me gay:
Since your return, the fun and moon
With brighter beams do fhine,
Streams murmur foft notes while they run,
As they did lang fyne.
Defpife the court and din of ftate;
Let that to their fhare fall,
Who can efteem fuch flavery great,
While bounded like a ball:
O'er moor and dale with
You may purfue the
And, after a blyth
All cares in my
And, in a vacant
You fhall be wholly
We'll make the bowers
And laugh at lang fyne.
The hero, pleas'd with the
The figns of gen'rous
Which had been utter'd
Bow'd to the pow'rs
Next day, with glad
Th' approach'd the
Where the good
And put them out
Should auld acquaintance be forgot,
And never brought to mind?
Should auld acquaintance be forgot,
And days o' lang syne!
Chorus
And for auld lang syne, my jo,
For auld lang syne,
We'll tak a cup o' kindness yet,
For auld lang syne.
We twa hae run about the braes,
And pou'd the gowans fine;

Thence country wives, wi' toil an' pain,
May plunge an' plunge the kirn in vain;
For oh! the yellow treasure's taen
      By witchin' skill;
An' dawtit twal-pint Hawkie's gane
      As yell's the bill.

Thence mystic knots mak great abuse
On young guidmen, fond, keen, an' crouse;
When the best wark-lume i' the house,
      By cantrip wit,
Is instant made no worth a louse,
      Just at the bit.

When thowes dissolve the snawy hoord,
An' float the jinglin' icy-boord,
Then water-kelpies haunt the foord,
      By your direction,
An' 'nighted trav'llers are allur'd
      To their destruction.

An' aft your moss-traversing spunkies
Decoy the wight that late an' drunk is:
The bleezin, curst, mischievous monkies
      Delude his eyes,
Till in some miry slough he sunk is,
      Ne'er mair to rise.

When masons' mystic word an' grip
In storms an' tempests raise you up,
Some cock or cat your rage maun stop,
      Or, strange to tell!
The youngest brither ye wad whip
      Aff straught to hell.

Lang syne, in Eden's bonnie yard,
When youthfu' lovers first were pair'd,
And all the soul of love they shar'd,
      The raptur'd hour,
Sweet on the fragrant flow'ry swaird,
      In shady bow'r;

Then you, ye auld snick-drawing dog!
Ye cam to Paradise incog.
An' play'd on man a cursed brogue,
      (Black be you fa!)
An' gied the infant warld a shog,
      'Maist ruin'd a'.

D'ye mind that day, when in a bizz,
Wi' reekit duds, an' reestit gizz,
Ye did present your smoutie phiz
       'Mang better folk,
An' sklented on the man of Uz
       Your spitefu' joke?

An' how ye gat him i' your thrall,
An' brak him out o' house an' hal',
While scabs an' blotches did him gall
       Wi' bitter claw,
An' lows'd his ill-tongu'd wicked scawl,
       Was warst ava?

But a' your doings to rehearse,
Your wily snares an' fechtin' fierce,
Sin' that day Michael did you pierce,
       Down to this time,
Wad ding a' Lallan tongue, or Erse,
       In prose or rhyme.

An' now, auld Cloots, I ken ye're thinkin',
A certain Bardie's rantin', drinkin',
Some luckless hour will send him linkin',
       To your black pit;
But faith! he'll turn a corner jinkin',
       An' cheat you yet.

But fare you weel, auld Nickie-ben!
O wad ye tak a thought an' men'!
Ye aiblins might - I dinna ken -
       Still hae a stake:
I'm wae to think upo' yon den,
       Ev'n for your sake!

DEATH AND DOCTOR HORNBOOK

Some books are lies frae end to end,
And some great lies were never penn'd:
Ev'n ministers, they hae been kenn'd,
       In holy rapture,
A rousing whid at times to vend,
       And nail't wi' Scripture.

But this that I am gaun to tell,
Which lately on a night befell,
Is just as true's the Deil's in hell
                    Or Dublin city:
That e'er he nearer comes oursel
                    'S a muckle pity.

The Clachan yill had made me canty,
I wasna fou, but just had plenty;
I stacher'd whyles, but yet took tent aye
                    To free the ditches;
An' hillocks, stanes, an' bushes kent aye
                    Frae ghaists an' witches.

The rising moon began to glowre
The distant Cumnock hills out-owre:
To count her horns, wi' a' my pow'r,
                    I set mysel;
But whether she had three or four
                    I cou'd na tell.

I was come round about the hill,
And todlin' down on Willie's mill,
Setting my staff, wi' a' my skill,
                    To keep me sicker;
Tho' leeward whyles, against my will,
                    I took a bicker.

I there wi' Something did forgather,
That pat me in an eerie swither;
An awfu' scythe, out-owre ae shouther,
                    Clear-dangling, hang;
A three-tae'd leister on the ither
                    Lay large an' lang.

Its stature seem'd lang Scotch ells twa,
The queerest shape that e'er I saw,
For fient a wame it had ava;
                    And then its shanks,
They were as thin, as sharp an' sma'
                    As cheeks o' branks.

'Guid-een,' quo' I; 'Friend! hae ye been mawin,
When ither folk are busy sawin?'
It seem'd to mak a kind o' stan',
                    But naething spak;
At length says I, 'Friend, wh'are ye gaun?
                    Will ye go back?'

It spak right howe – 'My name is Death,
But be na fley'd.' – Quoth I, 'Guid faith,
Ye're maybe come to stap my breath;
        But tent me, billie:
I red ye weel, tak care o' skaith,
        See, there's a gully!'

'Gudeman,' quo' he, 'put up your whittle,
I'm no design'd to try its mettle;
But if I did – I wad be kittle
        To be mislear'd –
I wad na mind it, no that spittle
        Out-owre my beard.'

'Weel, weel!' says I, 'a bargain be't;
Come, gies your hand, an' sae we're gree't;
We'll ease our shanks an' tak a seat –
        Come, gies your news;
This while ye hae been mony a gate,
        At mony a house.'

'Ay, ay!' quo' he, an' shook his head,
'It's e'en a lang lang time indeed
Sin' I began to nick the thread,
        An' choke the breath:
Folk maun do something for their bread,
        An' sae maun Death.

'Sax thousand years are near-hand fled,
Sin' I was to the butching bred;
An' mony a scheme in vain's been laid
        To stap or scaur me;
Till ane Hornbook's ta'en up the trade,
        An' faith! he'll waur me.

'Ye ken Jock Hornbook i' the clachan –
Deil mak his king's-hood in a spleuchan!
He's grown sae well acquaint wi' Buchan
        An' ither chaps,
The weans haud out their fingers laughin',
        And pouk my hips.

'See, here's a scythe, amd there's a dart –
They hae pierc'd mony a gallant heart;
But Doctor Hornbook, wi' his art
        And cursed skill,
Has made them baith no worth a fart!
        Damn'd haet they'll kill.

'''Twas but yestreen, nae farther gane,
I threw a noble throw at ane –
Wi' less, I'm sure, I've hundreds slain –
      But deil may care!
It just play'd dirl on the bane,
      But did nae mair.

'Hornbook was by wi' ready art,
And had sae fortified the part
That, when I lookèd to my dart,
      It was sae blunt,
Fient haet o't wad hae pierc'd the heart
      O' a kail-runt.

'I drew my scythe in sic a fury
I near-hand cowpit wi' my hurry,
But yet the bauld Apothecary
      Withstood the shock;
I might as weel hae tried a quarry
      O' hard whin rock.

'E'en them he canna get attended,
Altho' their face he ne'er had kenn'd it,
Just sh— in a kail-blade, and send it,
      As soon's he smells't,
Baith their disease, and what will mend it,
      At once he tells't.

'And then a' doctor's saws and whittles,
Of a' dimensions, shapes, an' mettles,
A' kinds o' boxes, mugs, an' bottles,
      He's sure to hae;
Their Latin names as fast he rattles
      As A B C.

'Calces o' fossils, earths, and trees;
True sal-marinum o' the seas;
The farina of beans and pease,
      He has't in plenty;
Aqua-fortis, what you please,
      He can content ye.

'Forbye some new uncommon weapons, –
Urinus spiritus of capons;
Or mite-horn shavings, filings, scrapings,
      Distill'd per se;
Sal-alkali o' midge-tail clippings,
      And mony mae.'

'Wae's me for Johnny Ged's Hole now,'
Quoth I, 'if that thae news be true!
His braw calf-ward where gowans grew
    Sae white and bonnie,
Nae doubt they'll rive it wi' the plew;
    They'll ruin Johnie!'

The creature grain'd an eldritch laugh,
And says 'Ye needna yoke the pleugh,
Kirk-yards will soon be till'd eneugh,
    Tak ye nae fear;
They'll a' be trench'd wi' mony a sheugh,
    In twa-three year.

'Where I kill'd ane, a fair strae-death,
By loss o' blood or want o' breath,
This night I'm free to tak my aith
    That Hornbook's skill
Has clad a score i' their last claith,
    By drap and pill.

'An honest wabster to his trade,
Whase wife's twa nieves were scarce weel-bred,
Gat tippence-worth to mend her head
    When it was sair;
The wife slade cannie to her bed,
    But ne'er spak mair.

'A country laird had ta'en the batts,
Or some curmurring in his guts,
His only son for Hornbook sets,
    An' pays him well:
The lad, for twa guid gimmer-pets,
    Was laird himsel.

'A bonnie lass, ye kenn'd her name,
Some ill brewn drink had hov'd her wame;
She trusts hersel, to hide the shame,
    In Hornbook's care;
Horn sent her aff to her lang hame,
    To hide it there.

'That's just a swatch o' Hornbook's way;
Thus goes he on from day to day,
Thus does he poison, kill, an' slay,
    An's weel pay'd for't;
Yet stops me o' my lawfu' prey
    Wi' his damn'd dirt.

'But, hark! I'll tell you of a plot,
Tho' dinna ye be speaking o't;
I'll nail the self-conceited sot
        As dead's a herrin':
Niest time we meet, I'll wad a groat,
        He gets his fairin'!'

But, just as he began to tell,
The auld kirk-hammer strak the bell
Some wee short hour ayont the twal,
        Which rais'd us baith:
I took the way that pleas'd mysel,
        And sae did Death.

The Auld Farmer's New-Year Morning Salutation to his Auld Mare, Maggie

ON GIVING HER THE ACCUSTOMED RIPP OF CORN TO HANSEL IN THE NEW YEAR

A guid New-Year I wish thee, Maggie!
Hae, there's a ripp to thy auld baggie:
Tho' thou's howe-backit now, an' knaggie,
        I've seen the day,
Thou could hae gane like ony staggie
        Out-owre the lay.

Tho' now thou's dowie, stiff, an' crazy,
An' thy auld hide's as white's a daisie,
I've seen thee dappled, sleek an' glaizie,
        A bonnie gray:
He should been tight that daurt to raize thee,
        Ance in a day.

Thou ance was i' the foremost rank,
A filly buirdly, steeve, an' swank,
An' set weel down a shapely shank,
        As e'er tread yird;
An' could hae flown out-owre a stank,
        Like ony bird.

It's now some nine-an'-twenty year,
Sin' thou was my guid-father's meere;
He gied me thee, o' tocher clear,
    An' fifty mark;
Tho' it was sma', 'twas weel-won gear,
    An' thou was stark.

When first I gaed to woo my Jenny,
Ye then was trottin' wi' your minnie:
Tho' ye was trickie, slee, an' funnie,
    Ye ne'er was donsie;
But hamely, tawie, quiet, an' cannie,
    An' unco sonsie.

That day ye pranc'd wi' muckle pride
When ye bure hame my bonnie bride;
An' sweet an' gracefu' she did ride,
    Wi' maiden air!
Kyle-Stewart I could braggèd wide
    For sic a pair.

Tho' now ye dow but hoyte and hobble,
An' wintle like a saumont-coble,
That day ye was a jinker noble
    For heels an' win'!
An' ran them till they a' did wobble
    Far, far behin'.

When thou an' I were young and skeigh,
An' stable-meals at fairs were driegh,
How thou wad prance, an' snore, an' skriegh
    An' tak the road!
Town's-bodies ran, and stood abeigh,
    An' ca't thee mad.

When thou was corn't, an' I was mellow,
We took the road aye like a swallow:
At brooses thou had ne'er a fellow
    For pith an' speed;
But ev'ry tail thou pay't them hollow,
    Where'er thou gaed.

The sma', droop-rumpled, hunter cattle,
Might aiblins waur'd thee for a brattle;
But sax Scotch miles, thou tried their mettle,
    An' gart them whaizle:
Nae whip nor spur, but just a wattle
    O' saugh or hazel.

Thou was a noble fittie-lan',
As e'er in tug or tow was drawn!
Aft thee an' I, in aucht hours' gaun,
      On guid March-weather,
Hae turn'd sax rood beside our han',
      For days thegither.

Thou never braindg't, an' fetch't, an' fliskit,
But thy auld tail thou wad hae whiskit,
An' spread abreed thy weel-fill'd brisket,
      Wi' pith an' pow'r,
Till spritty knowes wad rair't and riskit,
      An' slypet owre.

When frosts lay lang, an' snaws were deep,
An' threaten'd labout back to keep,
I gied thy cog a wee bit heap
      Aboon the timmer;
I kenn'd my Maggie wad na sleep
      For that, or simmer.

In cart or car thou never reestit;
The steyest brae thou wad hae faced it;
Thou never lap, an' stenned, and breastit,
      Then stood to blaw;
But, just thy step a wee thing hastit,
      Thou snoov't awa.

My pleugh is now thy bairn-time a',
Four gallant brutes as e'er did draw;
Forbye sax mae I've sell't awa
      That thou hast nurst:
They drew me thretteen pund an' twa,
      The very warst.

Mony a sair darg we twa hae wrought,
An' wi' the weary warl' fought!
An' mony an anxious day I thought
      We wad be beat!
Yet here to crazy age we're brought,
      Wi' something yet.

And think na, my auld trusty servan',
That now perhaps thou's less deservin',
An' thy auld days may end in starvin';
      For my last fou,
A heapit stimpart I'll reserve ane
      Laid by for you.

We've worn to crazy years thegither;
We'll toyte about wi' ane anither;
Wi' tentie care I'll flit thy tether
    To some hain'd rig,
Where ye may nobly rax your leather,
    Wi' sma' fatigue.

To a Mouse, On Turning Her up in Her Nest with the Plough, November, 1785

Wee, sleekit, cow'rin', tim'rous beastie,
O what a panic's in thy breastie!
Thou need na start awa sae hasty,
    Wi' bickering brattle!
I wad be laith to rin an' chase thee
    Wi' murd'ring pattle!

I'm truly sorry man's dominion
Has broken Nature's social union,
An' justifies that ill opinion
    Which makes thee startle
At me, thy poor earth-born companion,
    An' fellow-mortal!

I doubt na, whiles, but thou may thieve;
What then? poor beastie, thou maun live!
A daimen-icker in a thrave
    'S a sma' request:
I'll get a blessin' wi' the lave,
    And never miss't!

Thy wee bit housie, too, in ruin!
Its silly wa's the win's are strewin'!
An' naething, now, to big a new ane,
    O' foggage green!
An' bleak December's winds ensuin',
    Baith snell an' keen!

Thou saw the fields laid bare and waste
An' weary winter comin' fast,
An' cozie here, beneath the blast,
    Thou thought to dwell,
Till crash! the cruel coulter past
    Out-thro' thy cell.

That wee bit heap o' leaves an' stibble
Has cost thee mony a weary nibble!
Now thou's turn'd out, for a' thy trouble,
   But house or hald,
To thole the winter's sleety dribble,
   An' cranreuch cauld!

But, Mousie, thou art no thy lane,
In proving foresight may be vain:
The best laid schemes o' mice an' men
   Gang aft a-gley,
An' lea'e us nought but grief an' pain
   For promis'd joy.

Still thou art blest compar'd wi' me!
The present only toucheth thee:
But oh! I backward cast my e'e
   On prospects drear!
An' forward tho' I canna see,
   I guess an' fear!

ON GLENRIDDELL'S FOX BREAKING HIS CHAIN

Thou, Liberty, thou art my theme;
Not such as idle poets dream,
Who trick thee up a heathen goddess
That a fantastic cap and rod has:
Such stale conceits are poor and silly:
I paint thee out a highland filly,
A sturdy, stubborn, handsome dapple,
As sleek's a mouse, as round's an apple;
Who when thou pleasest can do wonders;
But, when thy luckless rider blunders,
Or if thy fancy should demur there,
Wilt break thy neck ere thou go further.

These things premised, I sing a Fox,
Was caught among his native rocks,
And to a dirty kennel chained, -
How he his liberty regained.

Glenriddell, whig without a stain,
A whig in principle and grain,
Couldst thou enslave a free-born creature,
A native denizen of Nature?
How couldst thou with a heart so good
(A better ne'er was sluiced with blood!)
Nail a poor devil to a tree
That ne'er did harm to thine or thee?

The staunchest whig, Glenriddell was
Quite frantic in his country's cause;
And oft was Reynard's prison passing,
And with his brother-whigs canvássing
The rights of men, the powers of women,
With all the dignity of freemen.

Sir Reynard daily heard debates
Of princes', kings', and Nations' fates,
With many rueful bloody stories
Of tyrants, Jacobites, and tories:
From liberty how angels fell,
And now are galley-slaves in hell;
How Nimrod first the trade began
Of binding slavery's chain on man;
How fell Semiramis (God damn her!)
Did first with sacrilegious hammer
(All ills till then were trivial matters)
For man dethroned forge 'hen-peck' fetters;
How Xerxes, that abandoned tory,
Thought cutting throats was reaping glory,
Until the stubborn whigs of Sparta
Taught him great Nature's *Magna Charta*;
How mighty Rome her fiat hurled
Resistless o'er a bowing world,
And, kinder than they did desire,
Polished mankind with sword and fire;
With much, too tedious to relate,
Of ancient and of modern date,
But ending still how Billy Pitt,
Unlucky boy! with wicked wit,
Has gagged old Britain, drained her coffer,
As butchers bind and bleed a heifer.

Thus wily Reynard by degrees,
In kennel listening at his ease,
Sucked in a mighty stock of knowledge,
As much as some folk at a College;
Knew Britain's rights and constitution,
Her aggrandisement, dimunition;
How fortune wrought us good from evil:
Let no man then despise the Devil,
As who should say 'I ne'er can need him,' –
Since we to scoundrels owe our freedom.

SCOTCH DRINK

Gie him strong drink, until he wink,
That's sinking in despair;
An' liquor guid to fire his bluid,
That's prest wi' grief an' care;
There let him bouse, an' deep carouse,
Wi' bumpers flowing o'er,
Till he forgets his loves or debts,
An' minds his griefs no more.
SOLOMON (Proverbs XXXI. 6, 7)

Let other Poets raise a fracas
'Bout vines, an' wines, an' drunken Bacchus,
An' crabbèd names an' stories wrack us,
            An' grate our lug;
I sing the juice Scotch bear can mak us,
            In glass or jug.

O thou, my Muse! guid auld Scotch Drink,
Whether thro' wimplin worms thou jink,
Or, richly brown, ream owre the brink,
            In glorious faem,
Inspire me, till I lisp an' wink,
            To sing thy name!

Let husky wheat the haughs adorn,
An' aits set up their awnie horn,
An' pease an' beans at een or morn,
            Perfume the plain;
Leeze me on thee, John Barleycorn,
            Thou King o' grain!

On thee aft Scotland chows her cood,
In souple scones, the wale o' food!
Or tumblin' in the boiling flood
        Wi' kail an' beef;
But when thou pours thy strong heart's blood,
        There thou shines chief.

Food fills the wame, an' keeps us livin';
Tho' life's a gift no worth receivin',
When heavy-dragg'd wi' pine an' grievin';
        But, oil'd by thee,
The wheels o' life gae down-hill, scrievin'
        Wi' rattlin' glee.

Thou clears the head o' doited Lear;
Thou cheers the heart o' drooping Care;
Thou strings the nerves o' Labour sair,
        At's weary toil;
Thou even brightens dark Despair
        Wi' gloomy smile.

Aft, clad in massy siller weed,
Wi' gentles thou erects thy head;
Yet humbly kind, in time o' need,
        The poor man's wine,
His wee drap parritch, or his bread,
        Thou kitchens fine.

Thou art the life o' public haunts;
But thee, what were our fairs and rants?
Ev'n godly meetings o' the saunts,
        By thee inspir'd,
When gaping they besiege the tents,
        Are doubly fir'd.

That merry night we get the corn in!
O sweetly then thou reams the horn in!
Or reekin' on a New-Year mornin'
        In cog or bicker,
An' just a wee drap sp'ritual burn in,
        An' gusty sucker!

When Vulcan gies his bellows breath,
An' ploughmen gather wi' their graith,
O rare to see thee fizz an' freath
        I' th' luggèd caup!
Then Burnewin comes on like death
        At ev'ry chaup.

Nae mercy, then, for airn or steel;
The brawnie, banie, ploughman chiel
Brings hard owrehip, wi' sturdy wheel,
                    The strong forehammer,
Till block an' studdie ring an' reel
                    Wi' dinsome clamour.

When skirlin' weanies see the light,
Thou maks the gossips clatter bright
How fumblin' cuifs their dearies slight –
                    Wae worth the name!
Nae Howdie gets a social night,
                    Or plack frae them.

When neibors anger at a plea,
An' just as wud as wud can be,
How easy can the barley-bree
                    Cement the quarrel!
It's aye the cheapest lawyer's fee
                    To taste the barrel.

Alake! that e'er my Muse has reason
To wyte her countrymen wi' treason;
But mony daily weet their weasan'
                    Wi' liquors nice,
An' hardly, in a winter's season,
                    E'er spier her price.

Wae worth that brandy, burning trash!
Fell source o' mony a pain an' brash!
Twins mony a poor, doylt, drucken hash,
                    O' half his days;
An' sends, beside, auld Scotland's cash
                    To her warst faes.

Ye Scots, wha wish auld Scotland well,
Ye chief, to you my tale I tell,
Poor plackless devils like mysel'!
                    It sets you ill,
Wi' bitter, dearthfu' wines to mell,
                    Or foreign gill.

May gravels round his blather wrench,
An' gouts torment him, inch by inch,
Wha twists his gruntle wi' a glunch
                    O' sour disdain,
Out owre a glass o' whisky punch
                    Wi' honest men!

O Whisky! soul o' plays an' pranks!
Accept a bardie's gratefu' thanks!
When wanting thee, what tuneless cranks
      Are my poor verses!
Thou comes – they rattle i' their ranks
      At ither's arses!

Thee, Ferintosh! O sadly lost!
Scotland, lament frae coast to coast!
Now colic-grips an' barkin' hoast
      May kill us a';
For loyal Forbes' charter'd boast
      Is ta'en awa!

Thae curst horse-leeches o' th' Excise,
Wha mak the whisky stells their prize –
Haud up thy hand, deil! Ance – twice – thrice!
      There, seize the blinkers!
An' bake them up in brunstane pies
      For poor damn'd drinkers.

Fortune! if thou'll but gie me still
Hale breeks, a bannock, and a gill,
An' rowth o' rhyme to rave at will,
      Tak' a' the rest,
An' deal't about as thy blind skill
      Directs thee best.

p. 89: The 'Auld Brig o' Doon', Alloway, near Robert Burns's birthplace.
p. 90: Near the village of Mauchline, Ayrshire, where Robert and his brother moved in 1784 to take over a farm.
p. 91: Lochlie, near the village of Tarbolton, the farm to which the Burns family moved in 1777.
p. 92: The public house in Ayr High Street, on which Burns probably based that visited by Tam in 'Tam o' Shanter', now a museum.
p. 93: The 'Auld Brig', Ayr.
pp. 94 and 95: Afton Water, Glenafton, Ayrshire.
p. 96: The coast near Alloway; the Heads of Ayr.

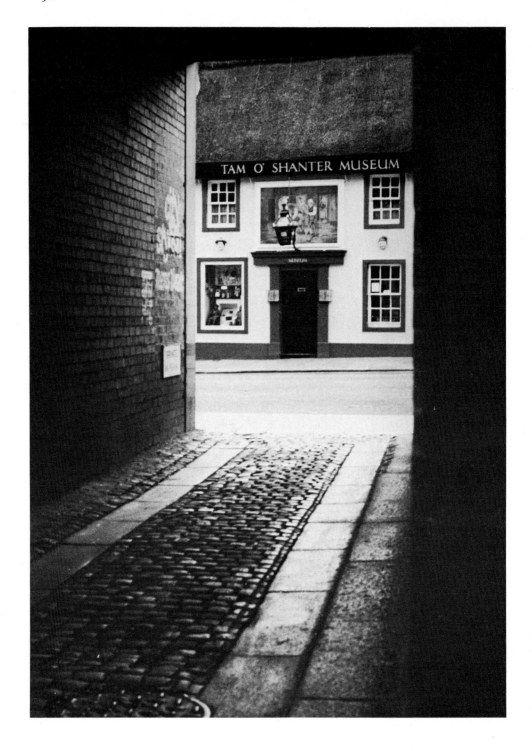

O WILLIE BREW'D A PECK O' MAUT

O Willie brew'd a peck o' maut,
   And Rob and Allan cam to see;
Three blyther hearts, that lee-lang night,
   Ye wad na found in Christendie.

We are na fou, we're no that fou,
   But just a drappie in our ee;
The cock may craw, the day may daw,
   And aye we'll taste the barley bree.

Here are we met, three merry boys,
   Three merry boys, I trow, are we;
And mony a night we've merry been,
   And mony mae we hope to be!

It is the moon, I ken her horn,
   That's blinkin' in the lift sae hie;
She shines sae bright to wyle us hame,
   But, by my sooth! she'll wait a wee.

Wha first shall rise to gang awa,
   A cuckold, coward loun is he!
Wha first beside his chair shall fa',
   He is the King among us three!

TAM GLEN

My heart is a breaking, dear Tittie,
   Some counsel unto me come len',
To anger them a' is a pity;
   But what will I do wi' Tam Glen?

I'm thinking, wi' sic a braw fellow,
   In poortith I might mak a fen';
What care I in riches to wallow,
   If I maunna marry Tam Glen?

There's Lowrie the laird o' Dumeller,
   'Guid-day to you, brute!' he comes ben:
He brags and he blaws o' his siller,
   But when will he dance like Tam Glen?

My minnie does constantly deave me,
    And bids me beware o' young men;
They flatter, she says, to deceive me;
    But wha can think sae o' Tam Glen?

My daddie says, gin I'll forsake him,
    He'll gie me guid hunder marks ten:
But, if it's ordained I maun take him,
    O wha will I get but Tam Glen?

Yestreen at the Valentines' dealing,
    My heart to my mou gied a sten:
For thrice I drew ane without failing,
    And thrice it was written, Tam Glen.

The last Halloween I was waukin'
    My droukit sark-sleeve, as ye ken;
His likeness cam up the house stalkin' –
    And the very grey breeks o' Tam Glen!

Come, counsel, dear Tittie, don't tarry;
    I'll gie you my bonnie black hen,
Gif ye will advise me to marry
    The lad I lo'e dearly, Tam Glen.

DUNCAN GRAY

Duncan Gray came here to woo,
    Ha, ha, the wooing o't,
On blythe Yule night when we were fou,
    Ha, ha, the wooing o't.
Maggie coost her head fu' heigh,
Look'd asklent and unco skeigh,
Gart poor Duncan stand abeigh;
    Ha, ha, the wooing o't.

Duncan fleech'd, and Duncan pray'd;
    Ha, ha, the wooing o't,
Meg was deaf as Ailsa Craig,
    Ha, ha, the wooing o't.
Duncan sigh'd baith out and in,
Grat his een baith bleer't and blin',
Spak o' lowpin o'er a linn;
    Ha, ha, the wooing o't.

Time and chance are but a tide,
      Ha, ha, the wooing o't,
Slighted love is sair to bide,
      Ha, ha, the wooing o't.
Shall I, like a fool, quoth he,
For a haughty hizzie die?
She may gae to – France for me!
      Ha, ha, the wooing o't.

How it comes let doctors tell,
      Ha, ha, the wooing o't,
Meg grew sick as he grew haill,
      Ha, ha, the wooing o't.
Something in her bosom wrings,
For relief a sigh she brings;
And O, her een they spak sic things!
      Ha, ha, the wooing o't.

Duncan was a lad o' grace,
      Ha, ha, the wooing o't,
Maggie's was a piteous case,
      Ha, ha, the wooing o't.
Duncan couldna be her death,
Swelling pity smoor'd his wrath;
Now they're crouse and cantie baith!
      Ha, ha, the wooing o't.

TIBBIE FOWLER

Tibbie Fowler o' the glen,
  There's o'er mony wooin' at her,
Tibbie Fowler o' the glen,
  There's o'er mony wooin' at her.

    Wooin' at her, pu'in' at her,
      Courtin' at her, canna get her:
      Filthy elf, it's for her pelf,
        That a' the lads are wooin' at her.

Ten cam east, and ten cam west,
  Ten came rowin' o'er the water;
Twa came down the lang dyke side,
  There's twa and thirty wooin' at her.

There's seven but, and seven ben,
  Seven in the pantry wi' her;
Twenty head about the door,
  There's ane and forty wooin' at her.

She's got pendles in her lugs,
  Cockle-shells wad set her better;
High-heel'd shoon and siller tags,
  And a' the lads are wooin' at her.

Be a lassie e'er sae black,
  An she hae the name o' siller,
Set her upo' Tintock-tap,
  The wind will blaw a man till her.

Be a lassie e'er sae fair;
  An she want the pennie siller;
A flie may fell her in the air,
  Before a man be even till her.

The Lass of Ecclefechan

Gat ye me, O gat ye me,
  O gat ye me wi' naething,
Rock and reel, and spinnin' wheel,
  A mickle quarter basin.
Bye attour, my gutcher has
  A heigh house and a laigh ane,
A' forbye, my bonnie sel',
  The toss of Ecclefechan.

O haud your tongue now, Luckie Laing,
  O haud your tongue and jauner;
I held the gate till you I met,
  Syne I began to wander:
I tint my whistle and my sang,
  I tint my peace and pleasure;
But your green graff, now, Luckie Laing,
  Wad airt me to my treasure.

John Anderson My Jo

John Anderson my jo, John,
  When we were first acquent,
Your locks were like the raven,
  Your bonnie brow was brent;
But now your brow is beld, John,
  Your locks are like the snow;
But blessings on your frosty pow,
  John Anderson, my jo.

John Anderson my jo, John,
  We clamb the hill thegither;
And mony a canty day, John,
  We've had wi' ane anither:
Now we maun totter down, John,
  And hand in hand we'll go,
And sleep thegither at the foot,
  John Anderson, my jo.

Auld Lang Syne

Should auld acquaintance be forgot,
  And never brought to min'?
Should auld acquaintance be forgot,
  And auld lang syne?

    For auld lang syne, my dear.
      For auld lang syne,
    We'll tak a cup o' kindness yet,
      For auld lang syne.

We twa hae run about the braes,
  And pu'd the gowans fine;
But we've wander'd mony a weary foot
  Sin' auld lang syne.

We twa hae paidled i' the burn,
  From morning sun till dine;
But seas between us braid hae roar'd
  Sin' auld lang syne.

And there's a hand, my trusty fiere,
    And gie's a hand o' thine;
And we'll tak a right guid-willie waught,
    For auld lang syne.

And surely ye'll be your pint-stowp,
    And surely I'll be mine;
And we'll tak a cup o' kindness yet
    For auld lang syne.

THERE WAS A LAD

There was a lad was born in Kyle,
But what'n a day o' what'n a style
I doubt it's hardly worth the while
    To be sae nice wi' Robin.

    Robin was a rovin' boy,
        Rantin' rovin', rantin' rovin';
    Robin was a rovin' boy,
        Rantin' rovin' Robin.

Our monarch's hindmost year but ane
Was five-and-twenty days begun,
'Twas then a blast o' Janwar win'
    Blew hansel in on Robin.

The gossip keekit in his loof,
Quo' scho, Wha lives will see the proof,
This waly boy will be nae coof,
    I think we'll ca' him Robin.

He'll hae misfortunes great and sma',
But aye a heart aboon them a';
He'll be a credit till us a',
    We'll a' be proud o' Robin.

But sure as three times three mak nine,
I see by ilka score and line,
This chap will dearly like our kin',
    So leeze me on thee, Robin.

Guid faith, quo' scho, I doubt you, Sir,
Ye gar the lasses lie aspar,
But twenty fauts ye may hae waur,
 So blessings on thee, Robin!

  Robin was a rovin' boy,
    Rantin' rovin', rantin' rovin';
  Robin was a rovin' boy,
    Rantin' rovin' Robin.

Green grow the rashes

  Green grow the rashes O,
    Green grow the rashes O;
  The sweetest hours that e'er I spend,
    Are spent amang the lasses O!

There's nought but care on ev'ry han',
  In ev'ry hour that passes O;
What signifies the life o' man,
  An' 'twere na for the lasses O.

The warly race may riches chase,
  An' riches still may fly them O;
An' tho' at last they catch them fast,
  Their hearts can ne'er enjoy them O.

But gie me a canny hour at e'en,
  My arms about my dearie O;
An' warly cares, an' warly men,
  May a' gae tapsalteerie O!

For you sae douce, ye sneer at this,
  Ye're nought but senseless asses O:
The wisest man the warl' saw,
  He dearly lov'd the lasses O.

Auld nature swears, the lovely dears
  Her noblest work she classes O;
Her prentice han' she tried on man,
  An' then she made the lasses O.

COMING THROUGH THE RYE

Coming through the rye, poor body,
　　Coming through the rye,
She draiglet a' her petticoatie,
　　Coming through the rye.

Gin a body meet a body
　　Coming through the rye;
Gin a body kiss a body,
　　Need a body cry?

Gin a body meet a body
　　Coming through the glen;
Gin a body kiss a body,
　　Need the world ken?

Jenny's a' wat, poor body;
　　Jenny's seldom dry;
She draiglet a' her petticoatie,
　　Coming through the rye.

---

p. 105: A portrait of Burns hanging above his writing desk in his house at Mill Vennel, Dumfries.
p. 106: Countryside near Dumfries, the market town where Burns worked as an excise officer.
p. 107: Sanquar Castle, in the uplands north-west of Dumfries.
p. 108: Fireplace and 'swee', or pivot, used to suspend pots over the fire, in the kitchen of Burns's Mill Vennel house.
p. 109: The bedroom at Mill Vennel where Robert Burns died on 21 July 1796.
p. 110: Ellisland Farm on the River Nith, which Burns took over in 1788.
p. 111: St Michael's Church, Dumfries, where Burns was buried.
p. 112: Robert Burns looks out over the Square in Ayr.

Lassie lie near me

Lang hae we parted been,
    Lassie my dearie;
Now we are met again,
    Lassie lie near me.

        Near me, near me,
        Lassie lie near me;
        Lang hast thou lien thy lane,
        Lassie lie near me.

A' that I hae endur'd,
    Lassie, my dearie,
Here in thy arms is cur'd,
    Lassie lie near me.

My love is like a red red rose

My love is like a red red rose
    That's newly sprung in June:
My love is like the melodie
    That's sweetly play'd in tune.

So fair art thou, my bonnie lass,
    So deep in love am I:
And I will love thee still, my dear,
    Till a' the seas gang dry.

Till a' the seas gang dry, my dear,
    And the rocks melt wi' the sun:
And I will love thee still, my dear,
    While the sands o' life shall run.

And fare thee weel, my only love,
    And fare thee weel awhile!
And I will come again, my love,
    Tho' it were ten thousand mile.

CA' THE YOWES

Ca' the yowes to the knowes,
Ca' them where the heather grows,
Ca' them where the burnie rows,
　My bonnie dearie.

Hark! the mavis' evening sang
Sounding Clouden's woods amang;
Then a-faulding let us gang,
　My bonnie dearie.

We'll gae down by Clouden side,
Thro' the hazels spreading wide
O'er the waves that sweetly glide
　To the moon sae clearly.

Yonder's Clouden's silent towers,
Where at moonshine midnight hours,
O'er the dewy-bending flowers,
　Fairies dance sae cheery.

Ghaist nor bogle shalt thou fear;
Thou'rt to love and Heaven sae dear,
Nocht of ill may come thee near,
　My bonnie dearie.

Fair and lovely as thou art,
Thou hast stown my very heart;
I can die – but canna part,
　My bonnie dearie.

OF A' THE AIRTS

Of a' the airts the wind can blaw,
   I dearly like the west,
For there the bonnie lassie lives,
   The lassie I lo'e best:
There's wild woods grow, and rivers row.
   And mony a hill between;
But day and night my fancy's flight
   Is ever wi' my Jean.

I see her in the dewy flowers,
   I see her sweet and fair:
I hear her in the tunefu' birds,
   I hear her charm the air:
There's not a bonnie flower that springs
   By fountain, shaw, or green;
There's not a bonnie bird that sings,
   But minds me o' my Jean.

O, WERT THOU IN THE CAULD BLAST

O, wert thou in the cauld blast,
   On yonder lea, on yonder lea,
My plaidie to the angry airt,
   I'd shelter thee, I'd shelter thee.
Or did misfortune's bitter storms
   Around thee blaw, around thee blaw,
Thy bield should be my bosom,
   To share it a', to share it a'.

Or were I in the wildest waste,
   Sae black and bare, sae black and bare,
The desert were a paradise,
   If thou wert there, if thou wert there.
Or were I monarch o' the globe,
   Wi' thee to reign, wi' thee to reign,
The brightest jewel in my crown
   Wad be my queen, wad be my queen.

TAM O' SHANTER

When chapman billies leave the street,
And drouthy neibors neibors meet,
As market-days are wearing late,
An' folk begin to tak the gate;
While we sit bousing at the nappy,
An' getting fou and unco happy,
We think na on the lang Scots miles,
The mosses, waters, slaps, and styles,
That lie between us and our hame,
Where sits our sulky sullen dame,
Gathering her brows like gathering storm,
Nursing her wrath to keep it warm.
    This truth fand honest Tam o' Shanter,
As he frae Ayr ae night did canter –
(Auld Ayr, wham ne'er a town surpasses
For honest men and bonnie lasses).
    O Tam! hadst thou but been sae wise
As ta'en thy ain wife Kate's advice!
She tauld thee weel thou was a skellum,
A bletherin', blusterin', drunken blellum;
That frae November till October,
Ae market-day thou was na sober;
That ilka melder wi' the miller
Thou sat as lang as thou had siller;
That every naig was ca'd a shoe on,
The smith and thee gat roarin' fou on;
That at the Lord's house, even on Sunday,
Thou drank wi' Kirkton Jean till Monday.
She prophesied that, late or soon,
Thou would be found deep drown'd in Doon;
Or catch'd wi' warlocks in the mirk
By Alloway's auld haunted kirk.
    Ah, gentle dames! it gars me greet
To think how mony counsels sweet,
How mony lengthen'd sage advices,
The husband frae the wife despises!
    But to our tale: Ae market night,
Tam had got planted unco right,
Fast by an ingle, bleezing finely,
Wi' reaming swats, that drank divinely;
And at his elbow, Souter Johnny,
His ancient, trusty, drouthy crony;
Tam lo'ed him like a very brither;
They had been fou for weeks thegither.
The night drave on wi' sangs and clatter;

And aye the ale was growing better:
The landlady and Tam grew gracious,
Wi' favours secret, sweet, and precious;
The souter tauld his queerest stories;
The landlord's laugh was ready chorus:
The storm without might rair and rustle,
Tam did na mind the storm a whistle.
    Care, mad to see a man sae happy,
E'en drown'd himsel amang the nappy.
As bees flee hame wi' lades o' treasure,
The minutes wing'd their way wi' pleasure;
Kings may be blest, but Tam was glorious,
O'er a' the ills o' life victorious!
    But pleasures are like poppies spread –
You seize the flow'r, its bloom is shed;
Or like the snow falls in the river –
A moment white, then melts for ever;
Or like the borealis race,
That flit ere you can point their place;
Or like the rainbow's lovely form
Evanishing amid the storm.
Nae man can tether time nor tide;
The hour approaches Tam maun ride;
That hour, o' night's black arch the key-stane,
That dreary hour, he mounts his beast in;
And sic a night he taks the road in,
As ne'er poor sinner was abroad in.
    The wind blew as 'twad blawn its last;
The rattling show'rs rose on the blast;
The speedy gleams the darkness swallow'd;
Loud, deep, and lang, the thunder bellow'd:
That night, a child might understand,
The Deil had business on his hand.
    Weel mounted on his gray mare, Meg,
A better never lifted leg,
Tam skelpit on thro' dub and mire,
Despising wind, and rain, and fire;
Whiles holding fast his gude blue bonnet;
Whiles crooning o'er some auld Scots sonnet;
Whiles glow'ring round wi' prudent cares,
Lest bogles catch him unawares.
Kirk-Alloway was drawing nigh,
Whare ghaists and houlets nightly cry.
    By this time he was cross the ford,
Where in the snaw the chapman smoor'd;
And past the birks and meikle stane,
Where drunken Charlie brak's neck-bane;
And thro' the whins, and by the cairn,

Where hunters fand the murder'd bairn;
And near the thorn, aboon the well,
Where Mungo's mither hang'd hersel.
Before him Doon pours all his floods;
The doubling storm roars thro' the woods;
The lightnings flash from pole to pole;
Near and more near the thunders roll:
When, glimmering thro' the groaning trees,
Kirk-Alloway seem'd in a bleeze;
Thro' ilka bore the beams were glancing;
And loud resounded mirth and dancing.
    Inspiring bold John Barleycorn!
What dangers thou canst make us scorn!
Wi' tippenny, we fear nae evil;
Wi' usquebae, we'll face the devil!
The swats sae ream'd in Tammie's noddle,
Fair play, he car'd na deils a boddle!
But Maggie stood right sair astonish'd,
Till, by the heel and hand admonish'd,
She ventur'd forward on the light;
And, vow! Tam saw an unco sight!
Warlocks and witches in a dance!
Nae cotillon brent new frae France,
But hornpipes, jigs, strathspeys, and reels,
Put life and mettle in their heels.
A winnock-bunker in the east,
There sat auld Nick, in shape o' beast –
A touzie tyke, black, grim, and large!
To gie them music was his charge:
He screw'd the pipes and gart them skirl,
Till roof and rafters a' did dirl.
Coffins stood round like open presses,
That shaw'd the dead in their last dresses;
And by some devilish cantraip sleight
Each in its cauld hand held a light,
By which heroic Tam was able
To note upon the haly table
A murderer's banes in gibbet-airns;
Twa span-lang, wee, unchristen'd bairns;
A thief new-cutted frae the rape –
Wi' his last gasp his gab did gape;
Five tomahawks, wi' blude red rusted;
Five scymitars, wi' murder crusted;
A garter, which a babe had strangled;
A knife, a father's throat had mangled,
Whom his ain son o' life bereft –
The gray hairs yet stack to the heft;
Wi' mair of horrible and awfu',

Which even to name wad be unlawfu'.
   As Tammie glowr'd, amaz'd, and curious,
The mirth and fun grew fast and furious:
The piper loud and louder blew;
The dancers quick and quicker flew;
They reel'd, they set, they cross'd, they cleekit,
Till ilka carlin swat and reekit,
And coost her duddies to the wark,
And linkit at it in her sark!
   Now Tam, O Tam! had thae been queans,
A' plump and strapping in their teens;
Their sarks, instead o' creeshie flannen,
Been snaw-white seventeen hunder linen!
Thir breeks o' mine, my only pair,
That ance were plush, o' gude blue hair,
I wad hae gi'en them off my hurdies,
For ae blink o' the bonnie burdies!
   But wither'd beldams, auld and droll,
Rigwoodie hags wad spean a foal,
Louping and flinging on a crummock,
I wonder didna turn thy stomach.
   But Tam kent what was what fu' brawlie,
There was ae winsome wench and walie
That night enlisted in the core,
Lang after kent on Carrick shore!
(For mony a beast to dead she shot,
And perish'd mony a bonnie boat,
And shook baith meikle corn and bear,
And kept the country-side in fear.)
Her cutty sark, o' Paisley harn,
That while a lassie she had worn,
In longitude tho' sorely scanty,
It was her best, and she was vauntie.
Ah! little kent thy reverend grannie
That sark she coft for her wee Nannie
Wi' twa pund Scots ('twas a' her riches)
Wad ever grac'd a dance of witches!
   But here my muse her wing maun cour;
Sic flights are far beyond her pow'r –
To sing how Nannie lap and flang
(A souple jade she was, and strang);
And how Tam stood, like ane bewitch'd,
And thought his very een enrich'd;
Even Satan glowr'd, and fidg'd fu' fain,
And hotch'd and blew wi' might and main:
Till first ae caper, syne anither,
Tam tint his reason a' thegither,
And roars out 'Weel done, Cutty-sark!'

And in an instant all was dark!
And scarcely had he Maggie rallied,
When out the hellish legion sallied.
   As bees bizz out wi' angry fyke
When plundering herds assail their byke,
As open pussie's mortal foes
When pop! she starts before their nose,
As eager runs the market-crowd,
When 'Catch the thief!' resounds aloud,
So Maggie runs; the witches follow,
Wi' mony an eldritch skriech and hollow.
   Ah, Tam! ah, Tam! thou'll get thy fairin'!
In hell they'll roast thee like a herrin'!
In vain thy Kate awaits thy comin'!
Kate soon will be a woefu' woman!
Now do thy speedy utmost, Meg,
And win the key-stane o' the brig:
There at them thou thy tail may toss,
A running stream they darena cross.
But ere the key-stane she could make,
The fient a tail she had to shake!
For Nannie, far before the rest,
Hard upon noble Maggie prest,
And flew at Tam wi' furious ettle;
But little wist she Maggie's mettle!
Ae spring brought off her master hale,
But left behind her ain gray tail:
The carlin claught her by the rump,
And left poor Maggie scarce a stump.
   Now, wha this tale o' truth shall read,
Each man and mother's son, take heed;
Whene'er to drink you are inclin'd,
Or cutty-sarks rin in your mind,
Think! ye may buy the joys o'er dear;
Remember Tam o' Shanter's mare.

Chronology

1757   William Burnes married Agnes Broun, 15 December.

1759   Robert Burns born at Alloway, 25 January.

1760   Gilbert Burns born. Other brothers and sisters were Agnes, Annabella, William, John, and Isabella.

1765   Robert and Gilbert taught by John Murdoch at the village school.

1766   Family moved to the farm of Mount Oliphant, near Alloway.

1768   Murdoch left Alloway. Robert and Gilbert continued their education under their father. Robert also helped on the farm.

1772   Robert and Gilbert sent to the parish school at Dalrymple for a few weeks before harvest.

1773   Robert studied English grammar and French for three weeks under John Murdoch in Ayr.

1774   Robert became his father's chief assistant on the farm. Paired at harvest with Nellie Kilpatrick, he wrote his first song, 'Handsome Nell'.

1775   Robert attended school at Kirkoswald to learn geometry, trigonometry and surveying.

1777   The family moved to the rented farm of Lochlie (Lochlea), near Tarbolton.

1780   With Gilbert and other local boys, Burns founded the Tarbolton Bachelors' Club.

1781   Burns joined the Freemasons and went to Irvine to learn the trade of flax-dressing. While here, he came across a copy of Robert Fergusson's poems which greatly influenced him.

1783   Burns commenced his First Commonplace Book containing 'Observations, Hints, Songs, Scraps of Poetry etc.'

1784   William Burnes died. The family moved to Mossgiel, and there followed on the poet's part a period of prolific output.

1785   Elizabeth, Robert's daughter by Betty Paton, born in May. Burns met Jean
        Armour.

1786   Burns planned to emigrate to Jamaica. Parted from Mary Campbell in May.
        Kilmarnock edition of his poems published 31 July. Invitation to Edinburgh to
        have another edition published caused Burns to abandon plans to emigrate.
        Twins, Robert and Jean, born to Jean Armour, 3 September.
        Burns arrived in Edinburgh in November. Burns's work favourably reviewed in
        The Lounger, and subscription bills were issued for the Edinburgh edition.

1787   Burns began his Second Commonplace Book, and the Edinburgh edition of his
        poems was published.
        Went on Border tour in May, and Highland tours in June and September.
        Burns met Mrs McLehose in Edinburgh.

1788   Burns left Edinburgh for Mauchline, 18 February.
        Jean Armour bore her second set of twins, 3 March – both dead within the
        month. Burns married Jean Armour in April and they set up house for a short
        time in Mauchline.
        Burns moved to the farm of Ellisland on the banks of the Nith near Dumfries
        in June and was made an excise officer.
        Jenny Clow bore a child to Burns in November.

1789   Francis Wallace Burns born. Burns took up duties as an excise officer, for £50
        per annum, to supplement his income from the farm.

1790   Burns completed 'Tam o' Shanter' in November.

1791   Daughter born to Anne Park in March; William Nicol Burns born in April.
        Burns gave up Ellisland, and moved to Dumfries to concentrate on his excise
        duties.

1792   Burns promoted to the Dumfries Port Division of the Excise in February, at £70
        per annum.
        Burns promised to contribute to Thomson's *Select Collection of Original Airs*.
        Elizabeth Riddell Burns born in November.

1793   Second Edinburgh edition of poems published in February.
        Family moved to Mill Vennel (now Burns Street), Dumfries, in May.
        Thomson's *Select Collection* published in June. Burns toured Galloway at end
        of July and beginning of August.

1794   James Glencairn Burns born in August.
        Burns promoted to Acting Supervisor in the Excise.
        This year also saw the last edition of his poems to appear in his lifetime,
        published in Edinburgh.

1795   Burns helped in organising the Dumfries Volunteers.
       Elizabeth Riddell Burns died in September.
       Burns himself became seriously ill with rheumatic fever in December.

1796   Burns died 21 July at his house in Mill Vennel and was buried in St Michael's
       churchyard, Dumfries.
       Maxwell Burns born on the day of his father's funeral.

Glossary

abeigh aside
aboon above
aft often
a-gley awry
aiblins perhaps
airn iron
airt direct
aith oath
aits oats
amaist almost
aspar legs apart
aucht eight
auld old
auld-light term in theological controversy, i.e. ultra-Calvinist
ava of all, at all
awnie bearded (of barley)
ayont beyond

baggie belly
bairn-time brood
barmie fermenting
batts colic
bear barley
belyve soon, presently
ben indoors, into the parlour
bicker short run; quarrel; wooden bowl
bide endure
bield shelter
big build
bill bull
billie friend
birk birch tree

bizz flurry
blae sharp
blate bashful
blather bladder
blellum babbler
boddle small coin
bogle ghost
boortree elder tree
bore chink
brae hill
braid broad
braindg't plunged
branks type of halter
brash short illness
brattle scurry, race
braxie sheep dead of a disease
breastit pressed forward
breeks trousers
brent smooth, unwrinkled
brisket breast
brogue trick
broose wedding race
brulzie uproar
brunstane brimstone
buirdly powerful
bum hum
bure sic hands fought so fiercely
bure the gree won first place
burn stream; water used in brewing
burnewin blacksmith
but into the kitchen or outer room

bye attour besides

caddie fellow
caird tinker
calf-ward churchyard
callan boy
cantraip (cantrip) magic, witching
canty cheerful
carl old man
carlin old woman
chap (chaup) knock
chapman pedlar
chiel fellow
chimla cheek fireside
clachan village; ale-house
clash gossip
clatter prattle
claught clutched
cleekit linked arms
cleg gadfly
clink money
clour bump
coft bought
cog wooden dish
coof (cuif) fool
cootie basin
cour fold
cowe humiliation
cowpit knocked over
cranreuch hoar-frost
creeshie greasy
crood coo
crouse cocksure
crummock crook
crunt blow on the head

curmurring rumbling
cushat ring-dove, wood-
  pigeon
cutty sark short shirt

daimen-icker occasional ear
  of corn
damn'd haet damned few
darg piece of work
dawtit cherished
deave deafen, annoy
diddle fiddle
ding beat
dinted pierced
dirl knock
doited confused
donsie unmanageable
douce decent, demure
dowie sad
draiglet draggled
driddle totter
driegh dreary
droukit drenched
drouthy thirsty
dub puddle
duds clothes
dusht butted

eild old age
elbuck elbow
eldritch eerie
ettle aim

faem foam
fairin deserts
fash bother
faulding folding
faut fault
ferintosh whisky with a
  peat-smoke flavour
ferly wonder
fetch't jerked
fidge fu' fain twitch with
  excitement
fient a the devil a
fient haet o't devil a bit of it
fiere comrade
fittie-lan' rear left-hand

horse in the plough team
fleech'd wheedled
fley'd scared
flingin' tree flail
fliskit fretted
foggage rank grass
forbye besides
fou drunk
freath froth
fyke commotion

gar make, cause
gate road
gear possessions
gied a sten gave a leap
gif if
gimmer-pet pet ewe
gin if
girnin' snarling; grinning
gizz wig
glunch scowl
govin' gazing vacantly
gowan daisy
graff grave
grain'd groaned
graith ploughing gear
grat wept
gruntle snout
guid-wullie waucht friendly
  drink
gully knife
gutcher grandfather

hain spare
haly holy
hand-waled hand-picked
hansel inaugural gift
hap trickle
harn coarse linen
hash good-for-nothing
haughs river meadows
hawkie cow
heckle flax comb
heeze lift
held my whisht kept silent
heugh pit
hingin' hanging
hirplin' hobbling

hissel flock of sheep
hizzie young woman
hoast cough
hog-shouther push about
hoodock hooded crow
hoolie! whoa!, slowly!
hotch'd fidgeted
houlet owl
hov'd caused to swell
howdie midwife
howe hollow
howkit dug up
hoyte waddle
hurdies buttocks
hyte mad

in a creel in confusion
ingle-cheek fireside,
  chimney corner
ingle-lowe firelight

jad jade
jauner chatter
jink dodge
jinker gay girl
jo sweetheart
jouk dodge
jundie jostle

keek peep
ken know
king's-hood paunch
kirn churn
kitchens serves as relish for
kittle inclined
kittle up tune up
knaggie knobbly
knowe hillock

lang syne long ago
lap leapt
lave the rest
lay pasture
lear learning
lee-lang life-long
leeze me blessings on
link skip
linn waterfall

lintwhite linnet
loof palm of the hand
loup jump
lowin blazing
lows'd loosened
lug ear
luggèd caup dish with handles
lume tool

mae more
maukin hare
maun must
maut malt
melder grinding of a customer's corn
men' mend
minnie mother
mishanter mishap
mislear'd unmannerly
mottie dusty
muslin-kail gruel

nappy strong ale
neuk nook
nieve fist

or before
owre over

pattle plough-staff
pawkie crafty, sly
pendle pendant
pickle a little
pintle penis
plack small coin
poortith poverty
pow head
preen pin
pyet magpie

quat quit
quean young girl

rair roar
ram-stam reckless
rash-buss clump of rushes
ratton rat

rax stretch
ream foam
red advise
reek smoke
reestit smoke-cured; frizzled
rief plunder
riggin rafters
rigwoodie wizened
ripp handful of corn
riskit made a tearing sound
rowth plenty

sark shirt
saugh willow
saumont-coble flat-bottomed salmon boat
scaud scald
scaur afraid
scawl scold
sconner feel sick
screed gash
scrievin' gliding
scrimpit stunted
scrimply barely
shaird shred
shaw thicket
sheugh ditch
shog jog
shoon shoes
sicker safe, steady
siller silver
simmer summer
skaith hurt
skeigh spirited
skellum scamp
skelpit spanked
skirlin' shrieking
sklented aimed obliquely, looked sideways at
skriegh scream
slap gap in a dyke
sleeest slyest
sleekit smooth
smeek smoke
smoor'd smothered
snell bitter
snick latch
snoov't moved smoothly

sonsie comely
sough sigh
souter shoemaker
spairges scatters about
spean wean; put someone off his food
speel climb
spence parlour
spier inquire
spleuchan tobacco pouch
splore hubbub
spritty full of rushes
spunkie will-o'-the-wisp
staggie young horse
stang sting
stark strong
staw stole
steer molest
steeve sturdy
stell still
stenned reared
steyest steepest
stick-and-stowe utterly
stimpart measure of grain
stoor gruff
stown stolen
strae-death natural death in bed
studdie stithy, anvil
sucker sugar
swank agile
swat sweated
swats new ale
swither uncertainty
syne since, then

tak tent pay attention
tapsalteerie topsy-turvy
tawie tractable
thairm fiddle-string
thole endure
thrang busily
thrave two stooks of corn
threap assert
three-tae'd leister three-pronged salmon spear
timmer wooden edge
tint lost

tirl strip off, unroof; twirl
tittie sister
tocher dowry
toss toast
touzie shaggy
toyte totter
trow trust
tug rawhide
tulzie wrangle
twal twelve
twins separates
tyke mongrel

unco very; strange

wabster weaver
wae worth a curse on
wale choice

wallop in a tether be
  hanged
wame belly
warly worldly
wat wet
water-brose meal and water
wattle twig
waukin watching over
waukit calloused
waukrife sleepless
waur overcome
weasan gullet
whid lie
whids frisks
whin gorse, furze
whittle clasp-knife
whyles at times
widdle struggle

wight stalwart
wimplin worm twisting
  spiral tube of a whisky still
winnock-bunker window
  seat
wintle roll; stagger
wud mad
wyle lure
wyte blame

yell milkless
yerkit stirred up
yestreen yesterday evening
yill ale
yird ground
yowe ewe